Interpreting the Lessons of the Church Year

m e s

LENT

PROCLAMATION 6 | SERIES A

FORTRESS PRESS | MINNEAPOLIS

Dedication

To the Congregations of
The Memorial Church,
Harvard University

Lively listeners, hopeful believers, faithful friends
For twenty-five years in a great and holy place they have granted me
the privilege of service as their
Pastor and Preacher

✝

This book is for them

PROCLAMATION 6
Interpreting the Lessons of the Church Year
Series A, Lent

Library of Congress Cataloging-in-Publication Data

Proclamation 6. Series A : interpreting the lessons of the church
  year.
       p. cm.
     Contents: [1] Advent/Christmas / J. Christiaan Beker — [2]
  Epiphany / Susan K. Hedahl — [3] Lent / Peter J. Gomes — [4] Holy
  Week / Robin Scroggs.
     ISBN 0-8006-4207-4 (v. 1 : alk. paper). — ISBN 0-8006-4208-2 (v.
  2 : alk. paper) — ISBN 0-8006-4209-0 (v. 3 : alk. paper) — ISBN 0-8006-4210-4
  (v. 4 : alk. paper)
     1. Bible—Homiletical use. 2. Bible—liturgical lessons,
  English.
  BS534.5P74 1995
  251—dc20   95-4622
                                                                       CIP

The paper used in this publication meets the minimum requirements of American National Standard for Information Sciences—Permanence of Paper for Printed Library Materials, ANSI Z329.48-1984. ∞™

Manufactured in U.S.A.   AF 1-4209

99   98   97   96   95   1   2   3   4   5   6   7   8   9   10

Contents

Preface

This is the third volume in the *Proclamation Series* on which I have worked, and I am pleased to be associated with so useful an enterprise.

I wish to thank my students in preaching, whose lively discussions have animated these pages; and I record with sincere appreciation my thanks to Eugene McAfee for his able assistance with the texts, and to Cynthia Wight Rossano for her excellent preparation of the manuscript.

I gratefully acknowledge the following for permission to use these materials in this volume: The excerpt from W. H. Auden's "For the Time Being" is from *W. H. Auden: Collected Poems,* copyright © 1942 and reprinted by permission of Random House, Inc. and Faber & Faber Ltd. The excerpt form e. e. cummings' "when god decided to invent" are reprinted from *Complete Poems: 1904–1962* by e. e. cummings, edited by George J. Firmage, by permission of Liveright Publishing Corporation; copyright © 1944, 1972, 1991 by the Trustees of the E. E. Cummings Trust.

P. J. Gomes

Introduction: The Uses and Needs of Lent

There is hardly a church in what we may still dare to call Christendom where some notice of Lent is not now taken. Perhaps an independent chapel or a charismatic congregation or two exists where the routine of Lent would continue to be thought of as popery; perhaps some of these would argue that the traditional themes of Lent, kept for a mere forty days, are in fact the substance of the daily work and worship of these traditions. It is not an exaggeration, however, to say that among American church-going Christians, and particularly among Protestants, Lent has become something of a serious season and one to be taken seriously.

This was not always so. Lent was "what Catholics did," in the opinion of the Protestant mainstream of not so long ago. Catholics "did it" together with high church Episcopalians and the odd Lutheran congregation. From my own youth I can recall the almost visceral objections we in the Protestant majority of my home town had to the "ostentatious display" the Catholics made of their ashes on Ash Wednesday. We knew that their priests kept them in ignorance of the Bible, yet somehow we expected them at least to appreciate the irony of their display, when Jesus himself, in Matthew 6:17-18, tells those who fast not to look dismal like the hypocrites, but "when you fast, anoint your head and wash your face, that your fasting may not be seen by men but by your Father who is in secret."

Our Catholic friends were always "giving up" something for Lent, or "doing something" for Lent, and we did not think much of their sacrifices in either direction. Then, of course, they would all insist upon having Good Friday as a day off from school. Had not both the Protestant Reformation and the American Revolution been waged to spare us all of this?

Good Protestants, particularly those of an evangelical flavor, would argue that the Lenten themes of personal piety, of the cross, the sense of sin, and the amendment of life, were indeed the themes that every Christian bore witness to on every day. No ordered season of reflection was necessary except perhaps in places where those themes were improperly neglected. The texts and subject matter of most Protestant hymn books of the first half of the twentieth century were almost wholly devoted to the life and work of Jesus, to his sacrifice and atonement, the struggle for personal salvation, and to Christian acts of charity, piety, self-denial, and prayer. Gospel hymns and the music of the black church were nearly always devoted to themes of atonement and personal salvation; and the musical piety of what we would now call "mainstream Protestantism" also reflected these concerns in the hymns on Sunday mornings, in the evening services, and in midweek meetings for prayer and instruction. The Wesleyan themes of personal holiness and sanctification, not yet confined to storefronts and televangelists, would be familiar to Protestants who sang the hymn of William D. Longstaff (1822–1894), *Take Time to be Holy:*

> *Take time to be holy, speak oft with thy Lord;*
> *Abide in Him always, and feed on His word.*
> *Make friends of God's children, help those who are weak;*
> *Forgetting in nothing His blessing to seek.*

The sense of retreat from the world, the wilderness experience from the temptation of Jesus in the desert, is invoked in the second stanza, where the Christian is invited to:

> *Take time to be holy, the world rushes on,*
> *Spend much time in secret with Jesus alone.*

Then at the end, the invitation to calmness of soul and submission as a foretaste of the world to come:

> *Take time to be holy, be calm in thy soul—*
> *Each thought and each motive beneath his control:*
> *Thus, led by his spirit to fountains of love,*
> *Thou soon shall be fitted for service above.*

In any survey of Protestant teaching in the nineteenth century it would be difficult to find much emphasis placed upon the liturgical season of Lent. Easter and Palm Sunday certainly are addressed; and few would fail to address the substance of Good Friday, although the day itself would not be kept in most Protestant circles until the first quarter of the twentieth century. The hymnody of Protestantism would articulate a theology of the cross and an anthropology of salvation waiting for a liturgical sensitivity to catch up with it. Isaac Watts (1674–1748), with his own superscription, "Crucified to the world by the Cross of Christ," set a high standard that has hardly been equaled, and never exceeded, in his gloss on Galatians 6:14, in the hymn we know as *When I Survey the Wondrous Cross.*

Long a staple in the Protestant armory of pious hymns, *When I Survey the Wondrous Cross* has an almost Roman fascination with the crucified savior and the physical reality of the cross. There is no aversion of the eyes here, no mere moral tale or fable, no hint of the heresy, Docetism, suggesting that the death of Jesus is a mere appearance; for in the third stanza the hymn requires the Christian to:

> *See from his head, his hands, his feet,*
> *Sorrow and love flow mingled down;*
> *Did e'er such love and sorrow meet?*
> *Or thorns compose so rich a crown.*

The most evocative of the hymns of the cross, composed originally as a catechetical hymn for Sunday School children, is that of Mrs. Cecil Francis Alexander, *There Is a Green Hill Far Away*. Generations have loved and have sung this narrative of the passion, although for many, "without a city wall" means, as it did for me in childhood, a wall-less city, a sylvan, suburban mound, and not the ash heap outside the city limits, literally beyond civilization. Nevertheless, the text is foundational in its description of the purpose of the Atonement found in stanza 3:

> *He died that we might be forgiven,*
> *He died to make us good,*
> *That we might go at last to heav'n*
> *Saved by his precious blood.*

No one else could do this, and with a succinct clarity dependent upon, but clearer than, the great works of Origen, Augustine, and Anselm, she goes on to say:

> *There was no other good enough*
> *To pay the price of sin;*
> *He only could unlock the gate of*
> *Heav'n, and let us in.*

The action is not one of judgment or of equity, but one of love that requires reciprocity. Even children understand this as fair, when Mrs. Alexander has them sing:

> *O dearly, dearly has he loved,*
> *And we must love him too,*
> *And trust in his redeeming blood,*
> *And try his works to do.*

Together with Isaac Watts and Mrs. Alexander must be joined the name of George Bernard (1873–1958), author of the hymn most frequently represented on lists of favorite American hymns of the twentieth century, *The Old Rugged Cross*. Hopelessly out of favor with the musically elite, and rather maudlin in its appropriation of the cross as a private totem, *The Old Rugged Cross* nonetheless must be acknowledged as a significant part of the public piety in helping to define Protestant Christianity in America. These three hymns represent but a small sample of a large and potent resource long available to the churches, and I would suggest that they form an underpinning, or skeletal, outline for the liturgical season of Lent. Lacking the organized devotional traditions of the Roman Church, American Protestantism appropriated its hymnody for this purpose, and thus, at one level at least, was equipped to embrace a season whose themes and rhythms were already familiar and graven upon the hearts of the faithful.

Lent, however, has more to it than hymnody and piety, important as these are. The uses of Lent are many, and the usage of the churches in recent years reflects this variety. An irony upon which I have earlier commented is that the rise in interest in Lent occurred just as the congregations of our churches were spending less and less time together in prayer, study, and worship. What was once the Protestant standard of Sunday school, Sunday morning and Sunday evening services, and a midweek meeting for prayer and study, was in steady decline by midcentury, and by the 1970s was nearly abandoned altogether by the mainline churches. Only in the South, among the Southern Baptists in particular, is one likely to see the old pattern still in place, and even there the evening service and midweek meetings are not now what they once were. In the growing independent church and family life movement, however, one sees a renewed emphasis upon multiple meetings of the congregation for worship and study. The discipline and inconvenience to the whole family of these gatherings over the week are regarded as marks of commitment, and an investment against the constant assaults and claims of the secular world.

Most churches today must place their entire reliance upon one occasion of Sunday worship, where now one twenty-minute sermon is expected to bear the burden of the entire Christian instruction that once was provided for adults through Sunday School, evening services, and midweek meetings, to say nothing of home study and private prayer. For many ministers, and indeed for some laypeople, Lent comes as an opportunity to take up an additional course of instruction and time for fellowship. What was once routine has now become extraordinary, and special services, series, and courses add flavor to the Lenten season. This is good. In my own congregation I have maintained this practice for many years. Any student of Lent, however, will be quick to note that Lent was meant to be a daily, weekday enterprise, and that Sunday was meant to be a relief from all of that and not, as is often the way today, a substitute for it. Thus the Sundays between Ash Wednesday and Palm Sunday, or the Sunday of the Passion, are historically known as Sundays *in* Lent, and not Sundays *of* Lent.

Comparison with the other penitential season, Advent, is instructive where the Sundays are *of* Advent, and the work of Advent is done on them.

The burden on the Sundays in Lent is considerable, and the pastor and congregation responsible for planning those Sundays, with the few hours available for the faithful, must work hard to take maximum advantage of the time allowed. In certain places the tradition of extra services, study programs, and corporate acts of discipline and reflection is regaining credibility, and fortunate is the pastor who has these resources upon which to draw. I have found great profit in taking a Lenten study series on one set of the lessons appointed for Lent, often using the *Proclamation Series* as one of my teaching and reference resources.

One year a series on the Lenten Psalms might be taught, and in another year, the Epistles or the Gospel lections; and sometimes these can be directly related to the sermon as a preaching and teaching dialogue. In other cases I have found to be equally helpful a Lenten study not directly related to the Sunday morning preaching. Some congregations follow the example of the Church of England, and have a "Lent Book," which is read and discussed over the course of the season. Other congregations experiment with various study-reflection-work projects of which Sunday worship is a part, but is not the whole enterprise. Still other churches, largely in urban areas, sponsor weekly and daily preaching missions during Lent. These were once very popular, often held at noontime or in the evening, and no preacher has ever been sufficiently stretched who has not been required to take a week or more of such duty.

When I was young, the "union service" was a popular Lenten device for ecumenically minded churches. On a Thursday evening during Lent each year, the Protestants would assemble in a different church, and the choirs and clergy would combine in worship with a visiting preacher from each denomination's hit parade. In some years one preacher would conduct the entire series. As a Baptist, I remember when Herbert Gezork, the charismatic president of Andover-Newton Theological School, and Samuel Howard Miller, the poetical dean of Harvard Divinity School, took their turn for Lent in the pulpit of our local church, thereby upholding the honor of the Baptists. In other years there would be a different preacher each week. This "union service" flourished for many years, but began to wither in the 1960s, along with so many institutional initiatives at that time, and it has never recovered its former energy.

Perhaps it is because there is so little time for Lent in these days that people are hungry for what time there is. In a world of less and less discipline, and in churches where spiritual hunger and thirst is of epidemic proportions, Lent presents itself as a natural and necessary season for focus and regrouping. In a way, its ancient mandate has been renewed. That mandate was to provide a season of preparation and instruction for those who wished to be baptized, instruction for those who wished to know how to become Christians, faithful followers of the risen Lord. They had something of the will for Christ, but they lacked discipline and knowledge, and could not get into the church without them. And so Lent became the season for the catechumens.

Most of the people I know in my own congregation and beyond know that they don't know what they need to know to be effective followers of Jesus Christ in the church and in the world. Many of them have a reservoir of personal piety, and a limited, attenuated Sunday school education upon which to build. They have a desire, a hunger even, to live spiritually satisfying lives, and they have some notion that it is the duty of the church to help them in this enterprise. Thus, surprisingly to many of the clergy, people are prepared to take Lent seriously if its obligations and opportunities are presented to them with clarity and conviction. Congregations are unusually attentive listeners during Lent, and these Lenten occasions are thus what the Pope once called "teachable moments." As pastors, preachers, teachers, and stewards of the mysteries of God, we should be prepared with all means at our disposal to take advantage of this susceptibility to the gospel.

This will mean taking more than the usual care in the preparation of our preaching. In Lent we have a double task. We have the text and texts to take seriously, we have the people and the occasion to take seriously, and somehow we must make the connection between the Word and the Season, and translate it into the needs and ambitions of the people. If this sounds manipulative, it is. But so is preaching. The texts and the occasions do not speak for themselves. If they did, they would not require our services and efforts. Rather than speak of manipulation, let us rather say that Lent should be orchestrated. The great themes have to be thought of, assembled, and organized; resources have to be identified and brought to bear, and the constituent parts need to be seen as of a whole, and leading to the great acts of Holy Week and Easter while still having their own integrity and identity. This means that neither preacher nor people should stumble into Lent unprepared.

Lent does not just happen. Lent requires the discipline not only of the pastor, but of the whole people, and part of that discipline in preparation consists of recognizing what cannot be done. Each Lent does not have to embrace every custom and expectation of Lent, just as every sermon in Lent need not embrace each of the lections provided. There have been some dreadful examples of homiletical stitchery in the effort to link all the lessons in one brilliant exposition, or to derive some hidden but universal truth that links them all together. Remember, heretical as it may seem in this publication, the lectionary was made for us, and not we for the lectionary.

Planning therefore is the key to Lent. What themes are to be given emphasis? What activities, in addition to Sunday morning worship, are to be contemplated? What is to be the relationship between preaching and teaching? How is Lent to be related to Holy Week and to Easter? What are the musical and liturgical resources to be enlisted? How can one best define this season for one's people in such a way that they can appropriate what they require for their own spiritual pilgimage throughout Lent?

All of this requires work. The effort that follows, at the highest of my ambitions, is to make that work easier, not to make that work less. It is for this reason that we will address issues of text, occasion, and some of the problems the conscientious preacher is likely to encounter with them. The discussion of the texts will cover necessary textual materials, leaving you to consult the usual helps of which there are many that are good and available. Not everything that can be said on these materials will be said, but issues that I identify as of basic importance will be addressed. My discussion of the texts is meant to be the beginning of, not the end of, your work. I will also from time to time say something about the particular liturgical requirements of the Sunday in question, as I am convinced that text and occasion are intimately related. Throughout, we are meant to deal with problems and opportunities for preaching; in other words, what can be done with any of this on Sunday morning. As the editorial board repeatedly emphasizes, these are not canned sermons. These are intended to launch you into your own ideas, perhaps in radical dissent from the views I present.

To preach the gospel in Lent is a wonderful opportunity, and no preacher could ask for more. This work is submitted in the hope that those who use it may find themselves refreshed and renewed in proclamation; enthusiastic, and better able to respond to those hungry sheep who look up, yearning to be fed.

Ash Wednesday
First Day of Lent

Lectionary	First Lesson	Psalm	Second Lesson	Gospel
Episcopal	Joel 2:1-2, 12-17 or Isa. 58:1-12	Psalm 103 or 103:8-14	2 Cor. 5:20b—6:10	Matt. 6:1-6, 16-21
Roman Catholic	Joel 2:12-18	Ps. 51:3-6, 12-14, 17	2 Cor. 5:20—6:2	Matt. 6:1-6, 16-18
Revised Common	Joel 2:1-2, 12-17 or Isa. 58:1-12	Ps. 51:1-17	2 Cor. 5:20b—6:10	Matt. 6:1-6, 16-21
Lutheran	Joel 2:12-19	Ps. 51:1-13	2 Cor. 5:20b—6:2	Matt. 6:1-6, 16-21

FIRST LESSON: JOEL 2:1-19; ISAIAH 58:1-12

The Roman Catholic, the Episcopal, and the Lutheran lectionaries, and the Revised Common Lectionary, are in remarkable agreement about what is to be read on the first day of Lent. The Episcopal and the Revised Common Lectionary provide the same alternate reading from Isaiah for the Joel lesson, and the Episcopal lectionary, alone among the others, departs from Psalm 51 in favor of Psalm 103.

The Joel passages would appear to be obvious. They discuss at verse 2 "a day of darkness and gloom, a day of clouds and thick darkness." A plague of locusts likened unto an army is about to beset the people and devour the land. Natural catastrophe is not merely nature at work, but is a sign of divine displeasure. The people, however, are given a chance to repent of the sins that have offended the Divine One, and, with the trumpet sounded, a solemn assembly is called to summon them to consider the approaching disaster. The disaster is the plague, and the prophets of that time are much like the American weather industry of today, with its ceaseless warnings of the approach of hurricanes and tornadoes. But their disaster is more than that: it is the approach of the Day of the Lord, the Day of Judgment when the judge shall find the people unprepared for examination. This is neither an army nor a plague, though metaphors for each are employed. This is the movement of time toward a people unprepared. The people do not move toward judgment, as has been the thinking of apocalyptic people since at least Augustine. No, here time, the Day of the Lord, moves toward the people like a tidal wave—to add yet another metaphor.

A word of warning is given to those who pray too freely for the coming of the Day of the Lord. At verse 11, the prophet notes that "the Day of the Lord is great and very terrible; who can endure it?" Judgment is not a beautiful thing: no one, no matter how virtuous or dutiful, can stand the scrutiny of God. The cry ought never to be for justice, but always for mercy; only arrogant Christians call for justice, always assuming that others will be judged and that they, somehow, will escape. Ash Wednesday and this passage remind the reader, in the words of another prophet: "for all have sinned and fallen short of the glory of God." Therefore everyone is under a judgment whereby he or she gets what they deserve, which is usually something other than what they would wish.

Joel creates a sense of natural inevitability. The meteorologist can predict and plot the oncoming storm but can do nothing to prevent it or to divert it from its chosen path. What has been set in progress cannot be abrogated. But, what is invariably true in nature is not necessarily true with God, which is why God should never be mistaken for the mere personification of nature, or of natural forces. " 'Yet even now,' " says the Lord in verse 12, " 'return to me with all your heart, with fasting, with weeping, and with mourning; and rend your hearts and not your garments.' Return to the Lord, your God, for he is gracious and merciful, slow to anger, and abounding in steadfast love, and repents of evil. Who knows whether he will not turn and repent?" (Joel 12:12-14, RSV).

The prophet holds out the possibility that if the people change, so too will God. It is not too late to alter the inevitable. This is the meaning of the Hebrew rendering in English, "Yet, even now." But, there are terms to this reversal. The people must wish it sincerely enough to acknowledge that they are the cause of the divine displeasure, they must repent of the part they have had in provoking it. Thus, to rend one's garments in the sign of sorrow and anxiety is not enough. The heart must be broken as well. Of the two emotions in play here, fear and sorrow, fear must yield to sorrow; and not merely sorrow at being caught, but sorrow at provoking God to such fearful judgment.

If that sorrow is serious and sincere, if the repentance of the people is genuine, who knows? Even God might repent. This is perhaps the most radical aspect of this passage, that God indeed might have a change of mind, heart, and will: "Who knows whether he will not turn and repent, and leave a blessing behind him, a cereal offering and a drink offering for the Lord, your God?" Genuine repentance from the people will provoke God to behave as is the nature of God, described at verse 13, as "gracious and merciful, slow to anger, and abounding in steadfast love." The prayer that Joel forms for the priests to say in the most public of places, "between the vestibule and the altar," is a prayer that the people, by their changed behavior and attitude, will allow God to be true to the divine nature, not vindictive and punitive, but gracious and full of love. The ultimate sin here will be for the behavior of the people to provoke God to place distance between the divine and the human, thus giving ammunition to those who are not the Lord's people, to say, "Where is their God?" Thus, repentance allows the people to be the people God meant them to be, and it allows God to be true to the divine nature. That is a powerful motivation for the amendment of life.

PSALM 51:1-17; 103

Psalm 51 is the classic invitation to personal renewal in the face of unpardonable sin. Nothing less than a new heart will do here, a new heart and a new attitude being necessary for the penitent to get on with a life worth living. The ultimate punishment is separation from God, estrangement and alienation. "Cast me not away from thy presence, and take not thy holy spirit from me," says verse 11 (KJV). Ancient commentary tradition ascribed this psalm to David, and his repentance of his sin with Bathsheba. The glory had departed from David, the apple of God's eye, and with a little help from the prophet Nathan, even David was made to see both the enormity of his sin and the enormity of its consequence for him and for his people. Nothing less than total renovation of spirit and life would do here. Again, the cry is for mercy, not justice. The divine standard is made clear: "Behold, thou desirest truth in the inward being" (v. 6). The transgression of that standard is acknowledged fully and freely: "For I know my transgression and my sin is ever before me; against thee, thee only have I sinned, and done that which is evil in thy sight" (v. 3). The divine sentence is just: "So that thou art justified in thy sentence and blameless in thy judgment."

Modern criticism halts at personifying this psalm in the character of David, but where is the harm in giving personality and character to the morphology of sin and repentance, which is clearly described in the psalm? Here the critical niceties, if observed too closely, get in the way, and are far less helpful than the question of Davidic authorship. Do *not* preach a sermon on whether David did or did not write this psalm. Who cares? The point is that to which the psalm points, and David's life is a useful lens with which to view that truth. The sense of sin that can no longer be rationalized or ignored, the desire for forgiveness against the standard of God, the nature of the God who can and who does forgive, and the response of the forgiven: these are lessons not to be minimalized or lost. What does the forgiven do? "Then will I teach transgressors thy ways, and sinners will return to thee." The forgiven becomes an evangelist, with the authority of his or her own forgiveness as the indisputable evidence of divine character. The result is not simply relief; the result is praise. "Oh Lord, open thou my lips, and my mouth shall show forth thy praise" (v. 15). The proof of forgiveness is not so much in the power of the forgiver, but in the unutterable joy of the forgiven.

The alternate reading in Psalm 103 places less emphasis upon the nature of the sinner, and more upon the nature of the God who forgives. This is a hymn to the one "who forgives all your iniquity, who heals all your diseases, who redeems your life from the Pit, who crowns you with steadfast love and mercy, who satisfies you with good as long as you live so that your youth is renewed like the eagle's" (vv. 3-5). The graciousness of God is the subject of Psalm 103: "For he knows our frame; he remembers we are dust" (v. 14). To those overwhelmed by the sense of sin—and we must never underestimate the power of the sense of sinfulness and unworthiness—the good news is the word of a gracious God whose property is to forgive, not out of necessity, but out of love. It was once thought that people had to be persuaded of their wickedness, confronted in the most vivid ways possible with their sinfulness. Those of us who have sat in the seat of counsellor with our people know that modern men and women are not lacking in a sense of sin. They know by bitter experience that they have "left undone those things which they ought to have done, and done those things which they ought not to have done." Indeed, the revised Episcopal Book of Common Prayer notwithstanding, there is no health in them. To such as these, and they are legion, forgiveness must be made as real and accessible as sin. Psalm 103 may help in that process.

SECOND LESSON: 2 CORINTHIANS 5:20—6:10

Is there life after repentance? St. Paul assures us that there is. In the Epistle for Ash Wednesday, 2 Corinthians 5:20—6:10, he invites the faithful to work together with God and to not accept the grace of God in vain. Repentance in this passage is a partnership: It is not God only who acts upon the sinner, but the sinner and God must engage together in the enterprise of grace. This cooperative nature of God encourages, indeed requires, a lively, mutually empowering action. Paul uses the language of reconciliation that implies the restoration of a fellowship which once was, and has since been broken by sin, recalling the estrangement of Joel and Psalm 51. It is the gracious God of Psalm 103 who is invoked by Paul at verse 3: "At the acceptable time I have listened to you, and helped you on the day of salvation." That "acceptable time," Paul argues, is now.

This reconciliation has already been achieved by the reconciling work of Christ, and as a result, as Paul points out in 5:16a: "From now on, therefore, we regard no one from a human point of view." This is a remarkable statement. The human point of view is one necessarily limited and limiting. It inhibits grace, it fetters the imagination, it makes one believe that the way he or she is is the way we are meant to be and must be. The human point of view limits both the human and the divine, and this gets in the way of the extraordinary transaction whereby grace gives new life to the dead before they die. But it will not work if it is only God's work. And it will not work if it is only the human enterprise. Now is the time to accept the grace of God, an acceptance that goes beyond conviction and confession. Nothing less that the amendment of life is at stake here, an enterprise that requires the mutual labor of the one who forgives and the one who is forgiven.

GOSPEL: MATTHEW 6:1-6

The Gospel reading from Matthew 6 starts out with the day's biggest problem. The day is called Ash Wednesday, and in most of our traditions the wearing of ashes is the primary liturgical feature of the day. Yet the first verse of the Gospel tells us: "Beware of practicing your piety before men in order to be seen by them; for then you will have no reward from your Father who is in heaven." We are invited in Scripture at a service of public worship to pray and to do our devotions and our good works in secret. We are encouraged by a negative example: do *not* do as the hypocrites, who love to be seen about their duties and devotions in public. For many, Matthew 6 is enough textual justification to do away with not only Ash Wednesday, but with all of Lent as well. Are we who do otherwise not flying in the face of Scripture itself?

It is important, indeed crucial, to realize that the keeping of Lent and the association of this text with Ash Wednesday is considerably older than American Protestantism's selective fascination with the literal sense of Scripture and the "doctrine" of *sola scriptura*. The apparent contradiction of liturgy and text has not remained hidden all these centuries just for us to discover; we must face the fact that there is something more here than a contradiction of text and practice, although it is that contradiction that will seize the attention of your people. Here is where it is a helpful practice to read the epistle before the Gospel in the liturgy, for by the epistle we are reminded that now, the "acceptable time" of which Paul speaks in Corinthians; now is the time that calls for a new order of everything, including a new order of piety, private and public, and a new form of prayer for people living in a world that is no longer to be viewed through human eyes alone. In this new order, old habits are done away with and are seen to be bankrupt and formless, seeking human approval and satisfaction rather than divine approbation. In the old form of prayer, the "human form," if you will, the focus was earthward, humanward: We were the subjects of our own discourse, the objects of our own prayer. We aspired to have our present condition improved, our dilemmas resolved, our needs satisfied. And we wanted credit for addressing these petitions to the divine. The public display of piety and contrition was meant to appease an appeasable God, or so it seemed.

But now—in God's now—the rules have changed. We are not meant to impress others. We are meant to address God. Harvard's venerable President Charles William Eliot was accused by his wife of mumbling Sunday's grace. "I couldn't hear you, dear," she remonstrated. "I wasn't speaking to you, dear," replied Mr. Eliot. We are not meant to mumble, but the direction of our prayer is inward and upward; and just so that we know how to do it properly, Jesus himself gives us a tutorial in prayer, the Lord's Prayer, whose direction and efficiency is not to be improved upon.

Matthew 6 introduces a new and impossible standard for Christian devotion in trying to get the self out of the center of the divine/human dialogue by placing the emphasis not on human treasure, which is subject to the corruption of the flesh, but on heavenly or divine treasure, which is forever. If we invest in heavenly treasure, that which the world can neither give nor take away, there too will our hearts be, in that place where true joys are surely fixed. Ashes remind us, if not others, of our mortality, of our bondage to the tyranny of the world as it is now, ruled over by death. Ashes are the human point of view. The ashes also remind us of that to which we aspire, that realm in which the Lord's Prayer is not impossible but is descriptive of the reality in which we believe; that now, that acceptable time, which by grace is available to us now.

THE OCCASION OF ASH WEDNESDAY

It is not necessary, and indeed it may prove unhelpful, to belabor your people with a history of Ash Wednesday. There are good and concise accounts of the origin of the day in a host of liturgical handbooks. The prudent minister should consult these and be prepared to answer the necessary and inevitable questions that people will ask, but do not risk the sin of telling them all that you know, which is usually considerably more than they need or want to know. You can address the history and rationale for Ash Wednesday in the materials you prepare well in advance of Lent for the instruction of your people. A pre-Lenten card or letter with a description of the season, something of its history and usage, and something of the expectations for all of the Lenten observances, is a useful thing to prepare and distribute in the weeks before Lent. Don't wait until the service to explain it. And if you are to employ the ancient custom of the imposition of ashes upon the foreheads of the people, make very certain that you have

prepared the people carefully and well in advance for this liturgical in-
novation, if it is such. If ashes are the "done thing" in your parish, well
and good: an explanation in advance is still probably in order. But if ashes
are a new thing with you, do not experiment on the day itself. Discuss the
liturgical history of the custom, relate it to the particular habits and style
of your worship, and by all means invite discussion in advance. Ash
Wednesday is not the day to play liturgical roulette with your people.
Prepare your people so that they will know what to expect. Some will not
want to come. Some will have liturgical phobias. It is better for them to
stay at home so that those who do come may have the full and informed
benefit of the liturgy.

The occasion itself is important, and not simply another opportunity for
preaching. It is important because it marks the beginning of a process, and
it must be seen as such and not as just another service, or as a liturgical
"extra." The connection of Ash Wednesday to the forty days of Lent, the
Sundays in Lent, and the solemnities of Holy Week, together with personal
participation in acts of self-denial, charity, private devotion, and the up-
building of private and corporate spiritual disciplines, needs to be made
explicit. We can assume the will of the people to take these matters up by
their presence at the liturgy of the day, whatever it may be. We may also
assume that they do not know how to activate their will in these matters,
and that they will need to be taught. What does the church expect of them?
What ought they to expect of the church, and of themselves? What is the
Lenten agenda, and how might they participate in it?

The Episcopal Book of Common Prayer, in its 1979 revision, produced
what I regard as a most helpful preface to Lent, to be read on Ash Wednesday
after the sermon. First the people are invited to the observance of a holy
Lent, and then follows an elegant and concise history of Lent, and an
invitation to a specific course of action that includes self-examination and
repentance, prayer, fasting, self-denial, and reading and meditating upon
God's holy word. The intention here is clear: It is to guide the people into
and through Lent by providing them with accessible forms of action and
reflection. Other traditions may wish to do this differently, but it must be
done. The focus is not backward, merely historical or antiquarian, but
forward, practical, applied, and therapeutic, rooted in the gospel, and
addressed to the human condition. An Ash Wednesday liturgy that is merely
historically or liturgically correct is an inadequate, even inappropriate
liturgy. If God is in the details, then the details of this occasion are neglected
at grave peril. This day may not be the day of your largest attendance; in
fact, the attendance, ever a Protestant fixation, may be quite small. The
preparation for and execution of the service nonetheless call for every

liturgical, pastoral, and homiletical skill of which you are capable. If Lent is to work well it must begin well, and it begins on Ash Wednesday.

Trust the texts, trust the occasion, trust the people, and trust the Spirit, but you must nevertheless work very hard to make some meaning of all of this, and the sermon or address on Ash Wednesday is a good place on which to focus that ambition. The problems are manifold and obvious. The day is provided with four incredibly rich and elusive readings, each one of which is fodder enough for a good sermon or for a whole series. The occasion itself is equally rich, and in some measure, ambiguous as well. For example, is the first day of Lent the beginning of a series of private spiritual journeys, Lenten twelve-step programs, as it were, for which the church is sponsor and of which you as preacher are ringmaster or therapist? Most people come to Lent because they have personal needs and personal journeys to make. How are we to reconcile, over the course of a liturgical season, those legitimate needs with the public and corporate needs of a worshiping congregation? For many there is an inevitable conflict between piety and activism, a false dichotomy that has done so much damage in this age to the witness of the Christian church. Lent seems to be the place where that conflict is played out in bold relief. How do we reconcile the old-fashioned claims of self-denial and abstinence in a world that denies these as virtues, in that same world that cries out for social justice and the restoration of a sense of common purpose and will? Can we afford to keep a holy Lent, and to "take time to be holy," while at the same time maintaining our hard-fought commitments to feed the hungry, house the homeless, clothe the naked, and work for a just moral and social order? Who is going to run the world, or the food cooperative, while we pray?

It will not do to pretend that these conflicts do not exist. We cannot wish them away for Lent. They will not disappear any sooner than will the "contradictions" of Matthew 6, and the customs of Ash Wednesday. These rough points, however, are points of entry and departure in preaching. The preacher should not try to make the rough places plain and the crooked straight. The people will detect any effort to skip lightly around these *impedimenta* to painless preaching. So, "hang a lantern on the 'problems,' " for that is where your listeners are. You don't have to solve them, at least not in one sermon on Ash Wednesday, but you ought to acknowledge a conundrum when you see one. The "safer" texts, those more user-friendly to the preacher, are of course the Psalm, and then perhaps in order, Joel, and, paradoxically, St. Paul. For once our prejudice against Paul and in favor of the Gospel will not this time protect us from a difficult or hard saying, but Matthew 6, set in the context of the other lessons, particularly 2 Corinthians, is, in my opinion, the place to spend one's time on Ash

Wednesday. If Lent is about renewal and the re-formation of both self and community, and it is, those elements are most vigorously addressed in Matthew 6. Setting an agenda for the accessible and the impossible in the Christian pilgrimage may indeed be just the right agenda for a Lent whose good news is to be found embedded in the verses of Matthew 6.

Don't, above all, try to explain everything. Resist the impulse to solve the gospel like a TV mystery. Leave something for the imagination, for study, for prayer, the Spirit, and the rest of Lent. Remember, you are getting your people started, not tidying up. Where the commentaries fail you, let the poets and the hymns help. T. S. Eliot's *Ash Wednesday* is by no means exhausted; and here is Robert Herrick's *To Keep a True Lent:*

> *Is this a fast, to keep the larder lean?*
> *And clean from vats of veal and sheep?*
> *Is it to quit the dish of flesh, yet still*
> *To fill the platter high with fish?*
> *Is it to fast an hour, or ragged to go,*
> *Or show a downcast look and sour?*
> *No: 'tis a fast to dole thy sheaf of wheat and*
> *Meat unto the hungry soul;*
> *It is a fast from strife and old debate, and hate,*
> *To circumcize thy life.*
> *To show a heart grief-rent;*
> *To starve thy sin, not bin;*
> *And that's to keep thy Lent.*

Prayer for the Preacher in Preparing for Ash Wednesday

O God, holy and eternal, who dost permit us to enter into the fellowship of that holy suffering by which thy dear Son, our Saviour, conquered sin and death; grant that we may celebrate the remembrance of his passion with true devotion, accept the cross as his disciples, and thus fulfill thy holy will; through the same Jesus Christ our Lord. Amen.

First Sunday in Lent

Lectionary	First Lesson	Psalm	Second Lesson	Gospel
Episcopal	Gen. 2:4b-9, 15-17, 25—3:7	Psalm 51 or 51:1-13	Rom. 5:12-19 (20-21)	Matt. 4:1-11
Roman Catholic	Gen. 2:7-9; 3:1-7	Ps. 51:3-4, 5-6, 12-13, 14, 17	Rom. 5:12-19 or 12:17-19	Matt. 4:1-11
Revised Common	Gen. 2:15-17; 3:1-7	Psalm 32	Rom. 5:12-19	Matt. 4:1-11
Lutheran	Gen. 2:7-9, 15-17; 3:1-7	Psalm 130	Rom. 5:12 (13-16), 17-19	Matt. 4:1-11

FIRST LESSON: GENESIS 2:4b-9, 15-17; 3:1-7

All of the traditions for which this series provides have chosen for today's first reading Genesis 2, and the second account of creation. Most of us were first introduced to biblical criticism when we discovered in the Book of Genesis that there were two accounts of creation. Hardly had the divine narrative begun when in the second chapter it repeated itself, but told the story in a different way. Most of us had not comprehended the notion of different biblical authors and audiences, and the discontinuities between the two accounts seemed annoying rather than profound or troubling. And yet an already confusing situation was made all the more so when we were taught in Old Testament 101 that the second account was more likely older than the first.

In this passage there are at least two subjects of more than passing interest, and we turn to these now. The first subject, strangely enough often neglected, is of God the creator. The creation, in all its myriad glory, is the work of God, what the Puritans delighted to call "God's handiwork," a work of art, of nature, and of pleasure. In our zeal to know more and still more about Adam and Eve, the geography of the garden, and the preexistence of the serpent, we tend to forget that the story is about God. God is the subject of Genesis. In the creation account we might ask, "What do we learn about God?" The writer wishes us to know that God is all there is, that it is God from whom all that is comes. The act of creation is in itself the ultimate exercise of sovereignty, the ultimate exercise of ultimate power. It is that power which the mad scientist of bad horror films craves, and when he achieves it in the "creation" of something or someone, he realizes how awesome and terrible that power is: there is none other like it. We learn about God in the creation saga, that, in the patristic aphorism, "He was when there was not." Creation itself is awesome. And if that is so, what can possibly be said about the creator of creation? So

many of us spend our time in trying to pick apart the details of the creation
story, or we try to make them conform to our own agendas and fail to
realize that at least part of the author's intent was to communicate the
intimate enormity of the creator-God, the God who made the earth and
the heavens, and whose own breath was breathed into the nostrils of the
dust creature and gave it life. The enormity of it all drives one to one's
knees. It also reminds one of the lines of e e cummings:

> *when god decided to invent*
> *everything he took one*
> *breath bigger than a circus tent*
> *and everything began*

An earlier generation would have remembered Ralph Waldo Emerson's
lines from *Woodnotes:*

> *Once slept the world an egg of stone,*
> *And pulse, and sound, and light was none;*
> *And God said, "Throb!" and there was motion,*
> *And the vast mass became vast ocean.*

The grandeur and glory of God, once the centerpiece of all Christian
theology, is not popular in modern thought. Perhaps the modern ego cannot
bear the comparison or the competition. One would hardly think of Genesis
2, that primary anthropological text, as having to do first and ultimately
with the nature of God, but first and last it *is* about God, powerful, creative,
and benevolent. There is no better place to begin in this text than with
God: in the beginning, God!

The second subject of interest is the creature, to whom E. A. Speiser
in his 1964 Anchor Bible commentary on Genesis 2, gave the title "earthling." Star Trek overtones of this designation notwithstanding, earthling
in fact is the best representation we have in verbal form of the relationship
between the creature and that substance out of which the creature is made:
out of the earth is made a creature of and for the earth. In Hebrew, the
etymological connection between creation and creature, and from which
the proper name Adam is derived, is clear. This is the import of
Genesis 2:7.

A careful reading of Genesis 2 will serve to correct some of our careless
assumptions about the order of events. First we note that the creature, the
earthling, is made out of the most basic stuff of the creation, dust. The
creature's life depends upon the breath of the creator. This first and basic
fact of our existence should serve as a corrective to an arrogant anthropology

that often deifies the human. We begin under the most modest of circumstances, created out of the most base of materials.

Second, the creation of the human occurs outside of the garden. Twice, at verse 8 and again at verse 15, the text takes pains to point out that the Lord placed the creature he had made into the garden he had made. We may view this placement as the second act of divine grace, after the creation itself. The garden, the Greek word for which is paradise or park, is the place where the creature is to fulfill its destiny. A rendering of the Hebrew at verse 15 is that the Lord took Adam and put him in, or caused him to rest in, the garden. Before the garden the creature has no purpose other than the divine pleasure. In the garden the creature has a vocation which is, at verse 15, "to till it and keep it."

This should cause us to reconsider our notion of "rest," "paradise," and "vocation." Rest does not mean the absence of labor. Rest here means purposeful exercise of one's skills in response to the will of God. Rest is the work of God. Thus, when heaven is described by Augustine and the other church fathers as a place of rest, they do not mean to suggest a place of idle retirement like some modern Sun City Senior Citizens' Home. They mean the place in which one does the work of God eternally. To do the will of God is that service which is perfect freedom. "Paradise," then, is that place of rest or work where one follows one's vocation, which is the will of God. The price of paradise is to do God's work and not our own, to follow God's will, and not ours.

Thus, these verses give us a fascinating sequence of the human enterprise. We are made out of the dust and outside of the garden. We are promoted into the garden where the terms of our presence there, the limits of paradise, are clear. The question is, can we stay? Then, of course, when we find it easier to follow our will rather than God's in paradise, we are returned to that place from which we have come, to what we might call mere living. It is almost an American story of rags to riches to rags, not in three generations, but in three chapters or so.

We should not anticipate the end of the story without a further consideration of the commandment by which the creature is forbidden to eat of the tree of the knowledge of good and evil. The price of happiness in paradise is obedience to this command, and obedience is based upon trust.

Here we have a problem, or at least a complication, for trust, if it is real, is based upon knowledge, and it is the tree of the knowledge of good and evil that is strictly off-limits to Adam. Verse 17 says, "but of the tree of the knowledge of good and evil you shall not eat, for in the day that you eat of it you shall die." The gospel hymn "Trust and Obey" seems to get it right when it says:

When we walk with the Lord in the light of his word,
What a glory he sheds on our way!
While we do his good will, he abides with us still,
And with all who will trust and obey.

The basis for obedience and trust here is the "light of his word." God has in many and various ways demonstrated trustworthiness. The word of the Lord is sure and good: the whole history of Israel is testimonial to this. The history of salvation is the evidence of the trustworthiness of God, and therefore we obey one whom we trust, and our trust is based upon the unambiguous and overwhelming evidence of the lovingkindness of the Lord. That is the *leitmotif* of the entire Psalter. That is the basis of Pauline preaching and teaching. But in the first days of creation, on what basis can poor Adam formulate his trust in God? He hardly knew God. How could he be expected to know God well enough to trust and hence to obey?

This kind of questioning, not unheard of among even casually literate listeners on a Sunday morning, may well force the preacher to address the fact that we do not read Genesis as if we do not know the rest of the story, and we do not read Genesis in the absence of our own images of God and what is appropriate godlike behavior. What is wrong with a healthy curiosity on the part of Adam about all of the trees in his new dominion? What is there about the knowledge of good and evil that will result in death? Is Adam promised death because, Prometheus-like, he gains a knowledge which will destroy him? Or is he promised death because in eating of the tree he will have disobeyed a direct command of God? Is the conclusion we draw here this: that it is better to be ignorant and alive than smart and dead? Are ignorance and innocence really the same?

We are of course not asking if this is true. We are asking the far more useful question: "What does this mean?" Limits in paradise is a theme which is suggestive for a season of self-reflection and examination in Lent. Even paradise is not all that it is cracked up to be; there are limits and risks there to be encountered at one's peril. Paradise takes many different forms, but in one respect all our paradises are the same: there are limits, bounds, and obstacles, and they exact a price. Preachers often preach about the sin of *hubris*, "pride," a Greek concept, which they argue is part of the landscape of paradise. They read our ego into Adam and ask, "Why not?" And Genesis becomes a Greek tragedy with its irony and inevitable doom. Indeed, death is introduced into the virginal creation by an insatiable curiosity about good and evil.

Perhaps this is not so much an invocation against pride as it is an invitation to modesty, the kind that says that "even within paradise there are limits upon the satisfaction of my needs and pleasures." Even in the company of one solitary Adam, there are limits and dangers. Henry David Thoreau said that he had three chairs in his simple hut in the wood at Walden Pond: "One for solitude, two for company, and three for society." Most of us would argue that trouble enters in at "society," and we uphold the virtue of the solitary, the individual, what Rheinhold Niebuhr once called "moral man and immoral society." Even before the other two chairs in Eden are filled by Eve and the serpent, we can see Adam and his problem. Where is paradise and what is wrong with it? might prove to be a useful question with which to consider this passage on the First Sunday in Lent.

PSALM 130; 32

The Roman Catholic and Episcopal lectionaries wisely revisit Psalm 51, perhaps on the assumption that the faithful will not have heard it on Ash Wednesday. The Lutherans call for Psalm 130, the *De Projundis*, with its cry of personal distress in confidence to a merciful God applied to the corporate condition of Israel. Personal distress and judgment yield to mercy and hope and redemption. The psalmists do not make light of trouble, and out of the depth, "thigh high," or "hip deep," in the rural vernacular, the cry is made. There is no sense here, unlike in Psalm 22, that the Lord has abandoned the petitioner or is indifferent. No, even in the depths the petitioner does not lose sight of the merciful and forgiving character of God. The petitioner is also aware that this call is a call for mercy and not for justice, for "If thou, O Lord, shouldst mark iniquities, Lord, who should stand?" (v. 3, KJV). Neither the reality of sin nor the justice of God is stinted, but neither of these inhibits the petitioner from sufficient confidence in the Lord in whom Israel hopes. Penitent people and penitent nations can each find it worthwhile to wait in expectation of the dawn of mercy. This psalm is discussed in more detail on the Fifth Sunday in Lent.

The Common Lectionary calls for Psalm 32, which rehearses the Ash Wednesday themes of confession of sin, forgiveness of sin, and amendment of life. The wicked whose pangs are many are those who do not confess their sin, who refuse to see themselves as they are. These cannot see God, and therefore cannot enjoy the bliss of forgiveness, for they have confessed to nothing. This was the Nixon pardon problem to many, for how could the late former President be pardoned when he had not confessed to any wrongdoing? This psalm begins with a clearer perspective on the subject: "Blessed," or as it is translated elsewhere, "Happy are those whose transgression is forgiven, whose sin is covered." The process of true confession, true forgiveness, and true amendment of life results in gladness. "Be glad in the Lord, and rejoice, O righteous, and shout for joy, all you upright in heart" (v. 11). We should hasten to remind ourselves and our people that the "righteous" and the "upright in heart" are people who confess their faults and are forgiven. They are not morally superior human beings, rather, they are beings whose self-confessed flaws are submitted to God, and who know the blessedness of being forgiven and of being given a new chance.

SECOND LESSON: ROMANS 5:12-19

All of the lectionaries require Romans 5:12-19 as the epistle reading on the first Sunday in Lent. Paul makes great use of the Adam/Christ typology, what Ireneaus called the Doctrine of Recapitulation, wherein what was in ancient times ruinous or problematic becomes under Christ redeemed and reformed. Irenaeus, expanding upon the example of Paul in Romans 5, constructs an elaborate process of recapitulation, whereby, for example, the tree of the forbidden fruit in the garden, the source of all our troubles, becomes the tree of redemption at Calvary upon which the second Adam, Christ, in perfect obedience gives life for death. Ireneaus has Mary's perfect obedience, as the handmaiden of the Lord, cancel out Eve's participation in the disobedience in Eden. The Garden of Eden, with its delights that harbor a sinister end in the serpent, is recapitulated in the Garden of Gethsemene, in whose darkness is harbored that ultimate submission of Jesus, the light of the world.

Paul is not simply being rhetorical here, although the device is very good rhetorically. He is being as practical and clear as he can be. The work of Christ, properly understood, has to be seen in its relationship to all that has preceded it. That work does not exist on its own *ex nihilo*. Christ is not simply the exception to all preceding history: he is the consequence and the corrective of all preceding history. Just as the world bore and bears the ineluctable mark of Adam, with its discourse of disobedience, denial, and death, so now the world bears the equally immutable mark of Christ with his claim to faithfulness, affirmation, and life.

Why does Christ do what he does? Because we need him to do so and cannot accomplish that work on our own. "While we were still weak," Paul says at verse 6, "at the right time, Christ died for the ungodly." Just as Adam did not "deserve" to be created, neither do we, the ungodly, "deserve" to be saved. It is the gracious act of creation and redemption that is at work here. As Mae West once said in another connection: "Goodness had nothin' to do with it." The work of Christ is a manifestation of the love of God. This is the truth of John 3:16, and we should remember that verse in this context as telling us almost all that we need to know about the character of God.

Paul is anxious here to make certain that we understand the work of Christ as part of the divine initiative, part of the divine plan for the redemption of the world. To look upon Christ as a tragic hero or as solitary martyr, a good man who gave up his life in the hope of doing some good, is to miss the point. For Paul, Christ's work is nothing less than God's design to reconcile the world to himself, and to do so in terms that we can understand, through a human life. Adam is used to explain who we are and how we have become what we are. Christ is used to confirm who we are meant to be and what in him we may become. Adam is an effort at explaining the problem of human identity, the will that refuses to be improved, the life that continues to be lost in mere living. Christ is offered by Paul as the solution to that problem, not by simply cancelling Adam out, but by giving to his descendants which precede and transcend death. This last point is one to which you may wish to return at Easter, namely, that one does not have to die to experience the new life in Christ, for in Christ there is life before death as well as after it. But we are getting ahead of our mandate. Certainly, however, the preacher will want to make some effort to link the Genesis lesson with this one. While not aspiring to the convoluted typologies of Ireneaus, the preacher may want to remind the readers and listeners that we look at Genesis now through the lenses of Paul. That will give them something to think about.

GOSPEL: MATTHEW 4:1-11

The lectionaries are unanimous in their provision of Matthew 4:1-11 as the Gospel reading for the First Sunday in Lent. From ancient times the account of the temptation of Jesus in the wilderness has been read as appropriate to the beginning of a season of spiritual discipline, self-denial, and prayer; and all of these occur within a context of temptation. As most preachers will be unable to resist the temptation to preach on the Gospel, we should spend some time on the issues it presents for the faithful and the curiously uninformed.

Perhaps the most striking thing of which to be reminded here is that this series of temptations follows immediately upon Jesus' baptism and the gift of the Holy Spirit. Matthew 3 concludes with an account of the baptism, the descent of the dove, and the pleasure God took in the baptismal act. The last words before the temptation are these: "This is my beloved son, in whom I am well pleased." What could be a more auspicious beginning to a new life?

Yet, the first encounter of the newly baptized is with Satan. Jesus does no good work, he performs no miracle, he is not granted a heavenly vision. He is led up, directed into the wilderness where he undergoes trial by ordeal. It is not a small thing to note that the context of the life of the baptized is a constant and ever increasingly sophisticated warfare with the devil. Baptism does not immunize one from temptation or from Satan: quite the contrary, it raises one's consciousness. The newly baptized meet temptations that they could not before even imagine.

This point may be salutary to those for whom Christian baptism holds still some magical power, and it may help them to understand that at baptism their troubles are only beginning. This will be less clear a point in those places where baptism has become simply a rite of passage, a naming ceremony, or an affirmation of the identity of the group into which the baptized is welcomed. In those places where something of the terror of the Christian profession is still expressed in the baptismal rite, however, the point will not be lost. Moviegoers will recall the opening scenes of *Godfather III,* where the baptism of the third generation of Corleones takes place against a montage of incredible Mafia violence of murder, gore, and assassination. The child is baptized into the very world his baptismal vows are meant to renounce. This is not mere irony or artfulness. The fallen world, with its inevitable and unavoidable sinfulness, is the context within which and against which one makes these solemn vows. It is for this reason that every teenaged confirmation or inquirers' class should be required to see *Godfather III* as a parable of life after baptism.

In the Episcopal Prayer Book of 1928, following an ancient formula the godfathers and godmothers are asked on behalf of the child:

> *Dost thou, therefore, in the name of this Child,*
> *renounce the devil and all his works, the vain*
> *pomp and glory of the world, with all the covetous*
> *desires of the same, and the carnal desires of the*
> *flesh, so that thou wilt not follow, nor be led by them?*

The answer is:

> *I renounce them all; and by God's help will endeavor*
> *not to follow, nor be led by them.*

Baptism may be an act of repentance, but it by no means assures the absence of that for which repentance is required. Instead of selling baptism as a user-friendly way to maintain and extend the church, we should be warning those who wish to be baptized, and those whom we wish to baptize, that life after baptism is full of "many dangers, toils, and snares." If they doubt you, or if you doubt the truth of this, read Matthew 3 and then read on directly into Matthew 4: the sequence is clear and unambiguous.

And so, if we learn first off that the consequence of baptism is conflict with Satan and with one's own self, for both are involved here in this account of our Lord's season in the wilderness, we learn also that the conflict cannot be managed on our own or with our own resources. This will be a helpful and necessary insight to those of your people who, in a fit of moral athleticism, have decided to break with their normal way of doing things, and either give up or take on something, or both, for Lent. Dieters and exercise faddists know the risks of attempted self-renovation by oneself. And, like the alcoholic, they know as well the terrible discouragement of "falling off the wagon." The novice moral athlete will attempt to make up for a lifetime of indulgence with a Lenten crash course in abstinence, and, when he or she inevitably fails and falls down, will think either themselves or the gospel impossible and inadequate. Oscar Wilde said, "I can resist anything but temptation"; and the town drunk said to his reformingly zealous wife, "I've fallen off more wagons than you've ever been on."

The new or renewing Christian will need to be reminded that the disciplines of Lent are not meant to demonstrate moral superiority, nor are they meant to secure divine or human approval. They are meant to toughen the soul. The faithful are to be reminded that these would-be solitary acts are not for oneself alone, but are for the well-being of the whole church. In other words, private virtue is a corporate act, and thus Lent is not meant to be carried on alone and in private. The Sundays in Lent and the extraordinary midweek occasions of devotion, study, and fellowship, are splendid opportunities for Christians to support and encourage one another in their Lenten work. Sharing one's ambitions and achievements, one's fears, failures, and frustrations ought not to be restricted to Alcoholics Annonymous and twelve-step programs. Such Lenten sharing, structured by the church as part of its Lenten program, ought to be seen as a part of the Lenten catechumenate designed to upbuild both the faithful and the community.

Three other points worth commenting upon in this account of our Lord's temptation are that (1) we should consider the nature of the wilderness, (2) we should take seriously the reasonable nature of the temptations, the suavity of Satan, if you will, and (3) we should consider how Jesus uses Scripture. Any one of these would make a splendid theme for Lenten preaching or a mid-week study course: all of them help us appropriate to the uses of our own Lenten agenda this account of Jesus' first great conflict.

For many, the wilderness is merely an alternative, and for some, an undesirable one, to the settled places of life. Wilderness may mean to some unspoilt mountain ranges, deep forests, and the places that L. L. Bean equips them to explore. For others, it may mean any place other than where they are. For still others, the wilderness is the very place from which they might wish to escape. We must not let our urban or suburban bias overwhelm us here.

For our purposes, let us at least initially think of wilderness as a place apart, any place other than where we usually are. Therefore a wilderness is not meant to be a miniature version of where we are, a camp with all of the comforts of home. For many of us, wilderness implies the disruption of the routine and the imposition, however temporary, of a new order, usually a simpler one. Lent gives permission for many people to go "into the wilderness," to simplify and clarify. In an undisciplined and overly demanding life, where most of us expect too much of ourselves and of others, permission to reorder and even to reduce some of those expectations, making more of less, may indeed come as a welcome opportunity. The church should help people to figure out how to do it. Corporate law firms hold "retreats," and industry encourages "focus groups": surely the community of Jesus, most especially in Lent, can rediscover the efficacy of the wilderness?

The suavity of Satan must never be underestimated. These temptations are all "reasonable." That is the ingenuity of them. Like all good temptations they tempt us to do the right thing for the wrong reason, or the wrong thing for the right reason. All of us wish to be good and to do good: That is our glory and our curse. And because we want to do the right thing we will be easily tempted to do anything. It is not our vices that will get us, but our virtues, and Satan is smart enough to know this. There is an aphorism, source unknown and hence available at will to everybody, which says that a surplus of virtue is more dangerous than a surplus of vice, because a surplus of virtue is not subject to the constraints of conscience. In the zeal for goodness, or the achievement of a good end, many on the way will be tempted to many wicked things. That is the stuff of drama and politics, and of human nature. It is the wide way down which Satan invites Jesus to travel, and it is an efficient and cost-effective way. Bread for stones is good economics, a demonstration of the effective power of God would save much preaching, and the delivery of the kingdoms of this world to Christ would spare us the need of evangelism. Few modern-day preachers would be able to resist all of that.

How did Jesus? He used Scripture. From this we learn that Jesus knew Scripture. He had read and studied his Bible. Even more to the point, we learn that Jesus knew that his situation was not unique. The devil had been at work before: these blandishments were not novel, not unique. They exist anywhere and everywhere the heirs of Adam try to make sense of their knowledge of good and evil on their own and by themselves. The Bible is a record of such encounters, and it provides counsel on how to cope with these matters. Jesus knew this and made appropriate use of what he knew.

THE OCCASION

Despite the liturgical precedence accorded Ash Wednesday, the First Sunday in Lent will be for most people the first opportunity to hear what Lent is about and what is in it for them. We know the paradox that makes of these Sundays intended as relief from Lent, the expression of Lent, and so we must take advantage of the paradox. There are some who will argue that all Sundays, those in Lent included, are festivals of the resurrection, and should always be kept as such. Even in the most observant of times, however, when Lent was a daily and not merely a weekly enterprise, the Lenten Sundays took on a different liturgical character. In these constricted secular days when we must do so much with so little, the case is even stronger for making of the Sundays in Lent something distinct from the other Sundays of the year. The churches who share this lectionary have wonderful resources at hand in liturgical vestments: the colors tell a vivid story, and those churches that still utilize the old-fashioned *Lenten Array* have an advantage meant for teaching. The character of the music can be of enormous significance here, and the liturgical emphasis upon confession and forgiveness can be utilized to great effect in this season. People are eager to be taught about Lent and are hungry for the symbolism and acts of worship that connect their personal pilgrimage to the great pilgrimage of the church. As leaders in worship we dare not let them down. On the Sundays in Lent, perhaps more than on the other Sundays of the year, God is in the details, so the preaching, teaching, and worship must be prepared with exemplary care.

Prayer for the Preacher in Preparing for the First Sunday in Lent

O God, by whose Spirit we are led into the wilderness of trial: grant us that standing in thy strength against the powers of darkness, we may so win the victory over all evil suggestions that with singleness of heart we may ever serve thee, and thee alone; through him who was in all points tempted as we are, thy Son, Jesus Christ our Lord. Amen.

Second Sunday in Lent

Lectionary	First Lesson	Psalm	Second Lesson	Gospel
Episcopal	Gen. 12:1-8	Ps. 33:12-20	Rom. 4:1-5 (6-12), 13-17	John 3:1-17
Roman Catholic	Gen. 12:1-4a	Ps. 33:4-5, 18-19, 20, 22	2 Tim. 1:8b-10	Matt. 17:1-9
Revised Common	Gen. 12:1-4a	Psalm 121	Rom. 4:1-5, 13-17	John 3:1-17 or Matt. 17:1-9
Lutheran	Gen. 12:1-8	Ps. 105:4-11	Rom. 4:1-5, 13-17	John 4:5-26 (27-30, 39-42)

FIRST LESSON: GENESIS 12:1-8

The lectionary unity continues in the first lesson for the Second Sunday in Lent, where all read in Genesis 12 of the call of Abraham. Last week it was God's work in Adam. Today it is God's work in Abraham. Last Sunday we noted that Adam was created after order had been imposed upon chaos. This week we note that Abraham is called out of a form of chaos, and from him will come order and promise. Between Adam and Abraham is life after the Fall, family troubles, conflicts, and the ambition, frustration, and confusion of the Tower of Babel. It may be said that in Abraham humanity gets a second chance. It may also be said that God gets a second chance as well, a re-creation, if not exactly a new one.

We first then consider the matter of choice. It is God who does the choosing, and the choice is Abraham, whose name, Abram, means "the father is exalted." To be exalted is to be chosen above others and set apart for a purpose. In the matter of choice the temptation is always to ask "why?" What are the credentials of the chosen one? What is it in the character of Abraham that God should choose him? Who is he, and what has he done to warrant the divine attention?

These are of course the wrong questions. Our meritocratic age will find it difficult to accept the fact that in God's choice of Abraham there is no merit at all. Abraham was not secretly good, his was not a virtue waiting to be discovered. This is no Victorian moral tale or Horatio Alger epic where the good are discovered and their goodness rewarded. First and last, this is an exercise of what Reformed theology delighted to call the sovereignty of God. It is God's will to exercise, and it is exercised in a summons to Abraham to "Go forth from your country and your kindred and your father's house to the land that I will show you." The summons is imperial, that is to say, it cannot be refused. There is no bargaining, no negotiation. The form does not say, "If you do these things I will bless you." It says,

"Do these things and I will bless you." Abraham is called by the same authority that created Adam out of dust and saliva. He is re-created here just as fully and functionally as Adam was when God breathed the breath of life into his nostrils. Now it is a bit more interesting in the consequence of this creation, this summoning forth, for a future is made explicit in the present. "And I will make of you a great nation," says God. Abraham will be a blessing, his name will be great, and all the nations of the earth will find in him their progenitor. Abraham becomes the means to God's end, a righteous and extended posterity.

It is no small ambition that God has in mind for Abraham. It is not clear that Abraham understands what he is in for. What is clear is that he does as he is told. He accepts the commission God places upon him, and the rest, as they say, is history. Abraham is called out of chaos for no apparent reason save that it is God who wishes him. He is not rewarded for past faithfulness. He is invested in for future promise. Neither credit nor glory belong to him: these belong to God. At this point our attention must not be on Abraham's faith in God, interesting and ultimately rewarding as that is. Our attention must be on God's faith in Abraham, unexpected, unearned, inexplicable.

This is a point worth pondering with the people of God. There is an old gospel hymn that says, in essence: "I can depend upon Jesus. Can Jesus depend upon me?" It is a fairly conventional thing, especially in Lent, to ask people to put their faith in God. "Let go and let God," we say. Perhaps it is a point of even greater wonder to ask how it is that God continues to place faith in the frail flesh of men and women who present no outstanding credentials, no great merit, no faith that God is bound to honor or to reward. Indeed, the faithfulness and obedience of Abraham are worth noting, and his place in the pantheon of faith is secure. We recognize this when we read in the great roll call of faithful heroes and heroines in Hebrews 11: "By faith Abraham obeyed when he was called to go out to a place which he was to receive as an inheritance; and he went out, not knowing where he was to go. By faith he sojourned in the land of promise, as in a foreign land." It goes on to say in Hebrews that Abraham "looked forward to the city which has foundations, whose builder and maker is God." (Heb. 11:8-10, RSV). What is it that causes God to place in an ordinary man his entire faith in the future? The implications of this exercise of God's faith in humanity, an anticipation of nothing less than the incarnation itself, are enormous for men and women who more often than not lack faith in themselves, and in a God who could choose them without regard to merit and worth.

Abraham had to hear that call before he could answer it. There is something to be said for listening for and responding to opportunity when it comes. What is it that the old business tycoons liked to say? Opportunity comes to the one who is prepared. There is something appealing about Abraham hearing God and knowing that the message was for him. God had to call the boy Samuel three times, and the boy heard only when the High Priest Eli told him to listen. The communication here is immediate and direct. We must give Abraham credit at least for being a good listener. What does he hear? An admonition to move forward and out into the future. The object of God's work is always ahead and beyond the people of God. Such faith is hardly conservative, backward-looking, or cautious. Faith is either future or nothing, and that is no choice, and the only choice.

PSALM 33

Let us confess in a spirit of Lenten candor that for most of us the Psalms are a problem. We do not know what to do with them. In many of our churches they are read in edited bits and pieces known as "responsive readings." In other places they are chanted or intoned with dreadful antiphons as if they could not stand up on their own. In some places, in the interest of time and the short attention span of modern Christians, they are eliminated altogether. At funerals we hear them, especially Psalm 23 and Psalm 139, as mantras of comfort, and for many of us the Psalms, especially those learned in our youth, form a permanent if eclectic part of our private devotions. But in church on Sunday mornings the psalms for most of us, in the churches of the United States, are a dead loss. There is no reason to believe that this is any less the case for the Psalms appointed for the Sundays in Lent, but in Lent we might undertake an effort to rehabilitate the Psalms for our public worship.

In all of Scripture the psalms are the most consistently honest dialogue between the human and the divine. They are pastoral and passionate. They are angry and loving. They exhibit fear and confidence. They portray an angry and jealous God who is the equal of any angry pagan deity, and they paint a picture of divine love as intimate as a shepherd and more faithful than the most constant friend. They reveal the gamut of human emotions, and thus they have more to say to us than the books of history, of prophecy, ethics, and doctrine. In those traditions where the whole Psalter is read through in some liturgical fashion, this incredibly rich panorama of the divine and human is taken into the hearts and minds of the faithful. In religious communities and in cathedrals, for example, the Psalter is designed to be heard daily throughout the course of a month. Twelve times the people share in this cosmic review. Most of us in these times, however, must be content with highlights and little bits.

In Lent, where the range of human emotion in divine worship is arguably greater than in other liturgical times, the Psalms can be a great asset to our worship. They pretend to no narrative, but they do allow us both to overhear and to enter into the most intimate of all conversations: those between God and the people of God. The Psalms, then, become the borrowed language of the faithful, a language belonging to another that is somehow and nevertheless our own. The people of that language, human and divine, are the people who share in the fate of Adam, the promises of Abraham, and now in the grace of God in Christ. For all of these people the Psalms are the language of the heart and therefore ought to be cherished as a gift of the spirit, as they give utterance when our own words are too woolly and those of others too removed from our own experience.

With these considerations in mind, the Psalms appointed for the Sundays in Lent should not be looked upon as so much filler, but rather as the binder that holds the other lessons together and allows us a form of spiritual ventilation when the historical books of Hebrew Scripture, the teachings of Paul, and, on occasion, even the words of the Gospels themselves sometimes are just too much—or too little—for us to take.

Today, because our lectionaries have no common mind on the Psalms for the Second Sunday in Lent, we have before us a range of expression and concern. The Roman Catholics and the Episcopalians have appointed Psalm 33, the Lutherans will read Psalm 105, and the Common Lectionary offers Psalm 121. In none of these will we find a hidden code or cypher by which to read the other lessons for the day; the seamless web of Scripture is not made easily manifest here. And yet these readings profit the people of God in their own right. The Lenten austerities would appear to be compromised by the opening of Psalm 33: "Rejoice in the Lord, O ye righteous!" Praise befits the upright. Psalm 105 is no less emphatic in its invitation: "O give thanks to the Lord, call on his name, make known his deeds among the peoples! Sing to him, sing praises, sing praises to him, tell of all his wonderful works! Glory in his holy name." Even the lovely restrained cadences of Psalm 121: "I will lift up mine eyes unto the hills," pulsates the convictions of one whose praise is the conviction that "The Lord will keep you from all evil; he will keep your life. The Lord will keep your going out and your coming in from this time forth and even for evermore."

These Psalms invoke our praise. In the midst of the Lenten wilderness they remind us of confidence, providence, and joy. The penitential quality of the season, even the quality of the so-called penitential psalms favored in Lent from ancient times, do not permit the faithful to forget even in Lent that the fundamental work of worship is praise. Liturgically, the people should have the Book of Psalms, and all of them, not just selected short subjects. For the preacher to preach on the psalms is to be able to stand on a high place from which it is possible to see with a clear eye the bright horizons of the two testaments. I commend to you C. S. Lewis's small book on the Psalms, and the Patristic and Reformed commentators on the Psalms will always repay the modern reader many times over. Protestant hymnody has a rich heritage in the use of the Psalms. The various psalters of the Scottish Church have given us great psalm paraphrases, many of which are to be found in a wide range of contemporary hymnals. Psalm texts in the textual and topical indices of hymn books as varied as *English Hymns Ancient and Modern Revised,* and John W. Peterson's American Singspiration Press, *Great Hymns of the Faith*, provide a rich repertoire for the careful planners of worship with Psalms.

SECOND LESSON: 2 TIMOTHY 1:8-10; ROMANS 4:1-17

The second lesson calls for 2 Timothy 1:8-10 for the Roman Catholics, and Romans 4:1-17 for the Episcopalians, Lutherans, and the Common Lectionary. The passage from Timothy offers words of encouragement from an older to a younger Christian engaged in the work of the gospel. The younger one is encouraged to not be inhibited by his youth or relative lack of experience, and he is urged to be unashamed of the one "who saved us and called us with a holy calling, not in virtue of our works, but in virtue of his own purpose," a theme wholly consistent with our earlier discussion of the call of Abraham. Our calling in God reflects more on God than it does on us, and thus to be ashamed of our calling is to be ashamed of God. Because God has confidence in us we too should have confidence, not only in God, but in ourselves, for together with God we do the work of God. Such a reading might appear to be reserved to those who have a vocation in the ministry and the priestly office, but no good Protestant would deny that all are called to the work of the gospel. This word of encouragement is not restricted to the clergy or to the professionals, but is essential to all. Such encouragement is not mere cheerleading: it is an act of empowerment for Christian people to get on with their work.

The Romans passage is Paul's treatment of Abraham's call, as he asks at the opening of chapter 4: "What then shall we say about Abraham, our forefather according to the flesh?" We know the answer. Abraham is not justified in being called of God by virtue of his works, for he had nothing to boast of before God. It was not superior merit that caught God's attention. God made the promise to Abraham, and Abraham believed that God would do as he promised. God's confidence in Abraham was vindicated by Abraham's confidence in God. The discussion of circumcision at verse 10 may seem as if Paul is off on one of his famous tangents, but the tangent does have a point. Abraham is circumcised after his call so that he can be reckoned the father of both the circumcised and the uncircumcised, and also to prove that he was set apart, "exalted," not by virtue of his circumcision, which would concede much to the circumcision party, but by virtue of God's call and his acceptance of it. It was faith, not the law, and not works, that made Abraham righteous. "That is why it depends on faith," Paul says at verse 16, "in order that the promise may rest on grace and be guaranteed to all his descendants—not only to the adherents of the law but also to those who share the faith of Abraham, for he is the father of us all." Paul, the apostle to the Gentiles, is not prepared to allow the Jews exclusive claim to Abraham. Paul affirms the inclusive nature of Abraham's patrimony so that the uncircumcised and those for whom the law is a stumbling block can respond in faithful righteousness to God's call even as Abraham did, and, indeed, *because* Abraham did: they and we are the legitimate seed of Abraham.

This is no small thing for contemporary Christians, who may think of Abraham as purely a "Jewish thing." The claim is that Abraham is the father of us all, and therefore God's call does not conform to the exclusivities of human invention but presumes a truly inclusive and boundaryless fellowship, the precondition for which is faith. Neither merit nor particularity, two errors as prominent now as they were among the readers of Paul's letters, are valid in assessing righteousness. Only faith counts, and Abraham is father of all the faithful.

GOSPEL: MATTHEW 17:1-9; JOHN 3:1-17; JOHN 4:5-30

The Gospel lessons present three quite different approaches to the question of the identity of Jesus. The Roman Catholics and the Common Lectionary both read Matthew 17:1-9, the account of the transfiguration, although the Common Lectionary has this as an alternate to its first choice of John 3:1-17, the account of Nicodemus, which also is the Gospel reading for the Episcopalians. The Lutherans provide John 4:5-30, the woman at the well, as their Gospel for the day. None of these admit of easy or simple treatment, although the familiarity of the John passage will make it seem the easier of the lot. The problem with such familiarity, however, is that it tempts preachers not to think, and congregations not to listen, and both lose.

All three of these are recognition stories, epiphanies of a sort, but in which the manifestation is not without effort, complication, and misunderstanding. Carefully considered, these three passages might be useful examples to thwart those who think it an easy thing to see Jesus and to know who he is at first sight.

The transfiguration is a vision of kingly glory, an experience that transforms the earthly teaching of Jesus into a vision of messianic glory. It will help to look at the parallel passages in Mark 9:2-8 and Luke 9:28-36 for more detail. Not only is Jesus seen in the vision, but so too are Moses and Elijah, the greatest of Israel's prophets. Moses is the lawgiver and the source of legitimate authority, and Elijah is meant to prefigure the Messiah. These symbols and signs would have been well known to any literate Jew. As if this is not enough to impress, there then is a voice from out of the cloud, repeating the baptismal blessing first heard at the beginning of Jesus' ministry. Mark records that Peter proposed to build three booths, or shelters, for Moses, Elijah, and Jesus, "for he did not know what to say, for they were exceedingly afraid" (Mark 9:6).

That Markan observation is a useful one, and we may avail ourselves of it even though our own pericope is far leaner because it exhibits a human response, identifiable in us all, to the *mysterium tremendum:* we start talking, and we want to do something. There are moments where there is no understanding or rational appropriation of the situation. There are times when the only response is to stand in silent, even ignorant, awe and adoration, and that is alright. We don't have to know or to understand everything. We don't have to explain everything or to make sense of it all. At the Mount of Transfiguration, both Peter and we can take profit from the modern aphorism: "Don't just do something: stand there." That will be very hard for us, for most of us prefer an explanation to the thing explained.

Nicodemus was a teacher in Israel, an intellectual, a wise and presumably good man, and certainly a cautious one. We can understand the secrecy of his interest in Jesus. He is also a man who appreciates a good explanation when he hears one. He is used to that, and that is why his interview with Jesus is so unsatisfactory. His questions make sense as one tries to develop the logic of an argument, but Jesus' impatience with him gets the better of good pedagogical method, and poor old Nicodemus is left in Jesus' rhetorical dust as we move on toward John 3:16.

Nicodemus, however, has captured the attention of many in the history of interpretation. Augustine saw Jesus as sympathetic to Nicodemus' inquiry, but for Augustine, Nicodemus was stuck at the literal sense of the text, and as a teacher in Israel he should have known better. Calvin had no patience with Nicodemus and thought him a proud man on whom Jesus was wasting his time. Matthew Henry points out that "Not many mighty and noble are called; yet some are, and here was one," and his charitable view of Nicodemus is justified by Nicodemus' later behavior when he defends Jesus, at John 7:50-52, and when, with Joseph of Arimathea, he confers upon Jesus the final dignity of burial after crucifixion. Henry Vaughan's poem *The Night* says of him:

> *Wise Nicodemus saw such light*
> *As made him know his God by night,*
> *Most blest believer he!*
> (David Lyle Jeffrey, *Dictionary of Biblical*
> *Tradition in English Literature,* 549)

It is easy to make a straw man, even a villain, of Nicodemus, and to use him as either a symbol of morally arthritic Judaism or the limits of an intellectual approach to faith. In yielding to this a great opportunity is lost. There are lots of secret disciples of Jesus who need their questions answered, and who themselves need to be taken seriously. John 3:16 applies to Nicodemus as much as to anybody.

The account of the woman at the well, in John 4:5-30, is impossible to treat as a whole in one sermon unless you are blessed with a seventeenth-century congregation prepared to listen long and well. In addition to its length, the story of the woman at the well enjoys a reputation for complexity second to few other discourses in the Gospels. Yet the themes of revelation and disclosure, and the wonderment and confusion they elicit, form the basis for this discourse.

The first thing to note is that Jesus is in conversation with a foreign woman. Two irregularities are present and at work here. The first is that Jews and Samaritans do not speak to one another. The strife between Palestinians and Israelis in modern times gives us a picture of the social tensions existing between Palestinians and Jews in New Testament times. They simply did not get along with one another. The second irregularity is that a Jewish rabbi is in a theological conversation with a woman. The fact that she is a foreign woman or a woman of allegedly loose morals is irrelevant. Rabbis did not engage in conversations with women at all.

So two taboos are broken at once. The inclusive patrimony of Abraham, of which we read in the Genesis lesson, and which Paul further develops in Romans, is here illustrated and amplified in the flesh and blood of the Gospel.

The encounter is initiated by Jesus. "Give me a drink," he asks of the woman as she is about to draw water for herself. She responds with the equivalent of, "you know better than that," and the conversation is off to a running start. The first section ends at verse 18, where the woman says, "Sir, give me this water, that I may not thirst, nor come here to draw."

The second portion extends from verse 16 to verse 26, where in a conversation about her husbands, she gives Jesus credit for knowing all things: "Sir, I perceive that you are a prophet" (v. 25). At the end of this portion she announces her belief in the Messiah and the nature of true worship, and Jesus proclaims that "I who speak to you am he."

The third section, at verse 27, begins with the return of the disciples and their surprise in finding Jesus in conversation with a woman. The woman, meanwhile, went out to tell her friends about Jesus. She returned, bringing many with her, and "many Samaritans from that city believed in him because of the woman's testimony" (v. 39). At verse 42 she recedes from the narrative.

The fourth section begins at verse 46. Jesus is asked to heal the son of an official. The gentile official affirms his faith in Jesus, and because of that faith Jesus heals the son.

These are all accounts of Jesus' encounters with people who for one reason or another are outside the circle of faith. The most radical of these is the encounter with the woman, whose circumstances are all transcended by Jesus. She becomes an evangelist and brings many to Christ. "The Samaritan woman," wrote Carol Newsome and Sharon Ringe in the *Women's Bible Commentary,* "is thus a witness and disciple like John the Baptist, Andrew, and Philip" (p. 296). The promise to Abraham is fulfilled.

Of all the disclosures in the Gospel passages made available for the Second Sunday in Lent, the one made to the woman at the well has the most immediate effect. On the Mount of Transfiguration, the Apostles, represented by Peter, are terrified and know not what to do. Nicodemus, his good intentions notwithstanding, has a hard time with the dialogue. But the woman at the well, once she gets it, goes out and proclaims it. An encounter with Jesus is not always an easy thing. People must be reminded of that. But there are moments of insight, of luminosity, when we see because we are seen. That, as Paul says, is an act of the grace of God.

Prayer for the Preacher in Preparing for the Second Sunday in Lent

Christ our God, who was transfigured upon the mountain, and who did manifest thy glory to thy disciples as they were able to bear it: shed forth thine everlasting light upon us, thy servants, that we may behold thy glory and enter into thy sufferings, and proclaim thee to the world. O thou who givest light in the darkness and art thyself the light of the world, Jesus Christ our Lord. Amen.

Third Sunday in Lent

Lectionary	First Lesson	Psalm	Second Lesson	Gospel
Episcopal	Exod. 17:1-7	Psalm 95 *or* 95:6-11	Rom. 5:1-11	John 4:5-26 (27-38), 39-42
Roman Catholic	Exod. 17:3-7	Ps. 95:1-2, 6-7, 8-9	Rom. 5:1-2, 5-8	John 4:5-42 *or* 4:5-15, 19-26, 39, 40-42
Revised Common	Exod. 17:1-7	Psalm 95	Rom. 5:1-11	John 4:5-42
Lutheran	Isa. 42:14-21	Psalm 142	Eph. 5:8-14	John 9:1-41 *or* 9:13-17, 34-39

FIRST LESSON: EXODUS 17:1-7; ISAIAH 42:14-21

Three of the lectionaries for this Sunday provide as the first lesson the account of the testing of God in the wilderness at Massah and Meribah, with the lesson ending at Exodus 17:7 with the question, "Is the Lord among us or not?" To the pious this may seem a rude, almost impertinent question, but at this telling of the story the children of Israel are in fact rude and impertinent. They are unhappy with Moses, and they are particularly unhappy with God, who seemingly led them out of Egypt to die of thirst in the desert. If this is salvation, then bondage is to be preferred. In another account of their unhappiness, in the chapter preceding this one, the children of Israel actually long for the flesh-pots of Egypt. We should note here that flesh-pot does not mean a place of sensual indulgence, as in a house of ill repute or an X-rated video arcade, but rather, dishes or pots of meat, the food of luxury and indulgence which was far more satisfactory to eat than the manna God provided in the desert.

These chapters in Exodus are designed to make explicit the difficult relationship between the people and God, and they do not paste over with a spiritual veneer these troubles and difficulties. When you are hungry and thirsty, you are your most vulnerable and cranky self, and metaphors and the remembrance of past favors simply will not do. It is easy for us to say that the children of Israel should have trusted in God. After all, did they not know that this was the same God who had brought them up out of the land of Egypt and destroyed their enemies, their horses, chariots, and riders, in the Red Sea? Are they not all, after all, children of promise, led by the cloud by day and the fire by night?

We may well think we know that, but it is clear from these chapters in Exodus that the children of Israel do not know, or if they do, they are not by that fact satisfied in their fundamental and immediate needs. "Is the Lord with us or not?" is to them a fair question, and we must honor it and not try to dismiss it. The wilderness is the place for such questions to arise.

We are tempted to turn the idea of the wilderness into a pleasant, even a pastoral, metaphor. I did so myself at the very first discussion of Lent, thinking of the wilderness as a place of retreat and contemplation, a place in which to be restored and to take a spiritual cure. Such a wilderness is not a bad place; it is benign, even benevolent. But before we domesticate the wilderness idea we should understand that in the Bible the notion of the wilderness is largely negative. There is something menacing about the wilderness, something raw and untamed, and in such a place basic fears and emotions flourish, and the wilderness becomes a place of temptation and testing. After all, when Jesus goes "on retreat" into the wilderness, he finds himself alone and with the devil. The wilderness, therefore, is not a suburban green space or a park. It is the place where those things we most fear and are least able to defend ourselves against are to be found in all of their fullness. For example, Numbers 20:5 calls the wilderness "this evil place"; and, in Deuteronomy 8:15, the wilderness is great and terrible, "with its fiery serpents and scorpions"; and in Deuteronomy 32:10, it is "a howling waste." The wilderness is where Cain is banished after the fratricide of Abel, and hence it is the place of outlaws and exiles.

Travelling through such a place to a distant destination, with the basic necessities of life such as water and food in questionable supply, is grounds for concern and complaint. The people think of themselves as neither unreasonable nor ungrateful, but for the moment they doubt that the situation is under control, they question the leadership of Moses, and they doubt, or fail to remember, the providence of God. "Is the Lord with us or not?"

This question is part of the "murmuring" of which Moses speaks at verse 4, when he says to God, "What shall I do with this people? They are almost ready to stone me." A long journey tests the fabric of the company making it. Chevy Chase's manic *Vacation* movies starring the Griswold family on its trip to Wally World, or through Europe, is the modern fable of this fact. "Are we having fun yet, are we there yet?" are the questions from the back seat of the car while the parents fiddle with the map. If Chevy Chase is not sufficiently sophisticated to make this point, there is W. H. Auden's account of the wise men's journey in pursuit of the star, where, in his Christmas oratorio, *For the Time Being*, he has the sages say:

> *The weather has been awful,*
>   *The countryside is dreary,*
> *Marsh, jungle, rock; and echoes mock,*
>   *Calling our hope unlawful.*
> ....
> *At least we know for certain that we are three old sinners,*
> *That this journey is much too long, that we want our dinners.*

The wilderness, therefore, is that difficult and dangerous place where not only the people are tested, but where the people test God. That is the point of the exercise at the encampment at Rephidim. The people wished to be reassured that they had not been abandoned, not led out of Egypt to die, not forsaken by the God who heretofore had done well by them. Such a wilderness place is the context for the miracle of the water from the rock. Moses asked, "Why do you find fault with me? Why do you put the Lord to the proof?" The people require more than a question for their answer, and the Lord provides an answer with the water from the rock. This should be the end of the matter, but it is not.

"Is the Lord with us or not?" We have heard this question in another form and in another wilderness earlier in our Lenten experience: "If you are the son of God, command these stones that they may become bread." It is a temptation of the first order to demand that God prove God's existence. God may be testing the people in the wilderness, but it is God who is tested by the people and who, with patience, love, and no small measure of exasperation, proves by providing. It was the impenitent thief, of whom we shall hear on Good Friday, who, in the same spirit of tempting God and demanding proof and satisfaction asked, "If you are the son of God, come down from the cross and save yourself and us."

We know these questions in our own spiritual wilderness. If you are God, save my marriage, cure my cancer, restore my lost fortunes, protect my children, help me get that contract, help me beat the odds. It does not matter what acts of faithfulness, mercy, and providence occurred in the past. It does not matter what you did for my ancestors, my parents, or even myself just yesterday. "Is the Lord with us or not?"

PSALM 95

The point of Psalm 95 is to remind us that we tempt God. We would-be believers do it all the time. We demand proof and immediate satisfaction and gratification from God at the very moment that we forget what God has already done for us. Psalm 95 is more about amnesia than it is about praise. We are so obsessed by our present anxieties and discontents, overwhelmed by our circumstances and inconveniences, diverted by our doubts and necessities, that we are momentarily blinded to what God has already done for us, is doing for us, and will do for us. The psalm reminds us that the context of praise is not petition but rather remembrance and thanksgiving for the faithfulness of God. Verses 1–7 are a hymn of praise for the attributes of God: "For the Lord is a great God, and a great king above all gods." The faithful need to be reminded of the faithfulness of God. The remembrance of that faithfulness is all the more important when, in the profitable words of Harold Kushner's useful book, "bad things happen to good people."

Most religious people believe themselves to be the "good people" to whom "bad things" happen. Their logic is that God has forgotten just how good they are, otherwise these "bad things" would not have happened to them, but rather to somebody else, a "bad" person who deserved the distress and sorrow. The cult of victimhood is not new. It is as old as Meribah and Massah, and the murmurings at Rephidim. But the psalm argues in its transition at verse 8 that we should not become the victims of our own victimhood. "O that today you would hearken to his voice." O that today you would actually listen and hear the Lord, and not merely the echoes of your own discontent. The mood has changed within the psalm. The first verses might well be of the ordinary singer of songs of praise, but at verse 8 the entreaty, as it were, is from the very soul of God. "Do not harden your hearts against me as at Meribah, as on the day at Massah in the wilderness, when your fathers tested me and put me to the proof, though they had seen my work." If you detect a tone of irritation in the God voice here, you are right, for God is mightily annoyed at those who doubt and test the divine faithfulness, especially in the face of so many proofs, which the people conveniently had forgot. We get a taste of the anger of God at such faithfulness: "For forty years I loathed that generation and said, 'they are a people who err in heart, and they do not regard my ways.' Therefore I swore in my anger that they should not enter into my rest."

SECOND LESSON: ROMANS 5:1-14

The faithfulness of God, the insecurity of the people, and indeed the repentance of God for his own annoyance at his ungrateful people, are great themes that unite the Psalm and the lesson from Exodus. A theme of great interest as well is the rock itself, and the water that issued forth from it at the command of Moses. Refreshment from an unyielding or unpromising source, the comparison between the hard stone and the flowing water, and the power or authority that would command the stone to yield water, are all useful subjects to pursue. The episode is recapitulated in Numbers 20:1-13, and St. Paul refers to this incident when, in 2 Corinthians 10:4, he says of the Jews, "They did all drink of the same spiritual drink; for they drank of that spiritual rock that followed them, and that rock was Christ." William Williams' hymn, *"Guide Me, O Thou Great Jehovah, Pilgrim Through This Barren Land,"* takes this episode in the wilderness as its basis. Perhaps the most famous allusion to the text is in Augustus Montague Toplady's hymn, *"Rock of Ages, Cleft for Me."* Here, with the liberty of the figural poet, the rock has become a figure of Christ and the striking of it a sacramental act. Thus the rock that in some sense was a symbol of God's response to a faithless people, becomes for the faithless people an act of atonement and an ultimate reconciliation with God. The seventeenth-century English poet, Richard Crashaw, makes of the rock a symbol for the rock-hewn tomb of Christ, and the water that comes from the rock is both Christ and immortality for those who believe. The sacramental and eucharistic similes and metaphors of water from the rock, and the satisfaction of the thirst of the people by an act of God have not been lost upon the poets and writers of hymns.

Romans 5 is Paul's great chapter on justification by faith, and an unambiguous rebuke to the anxieties and hardness of heart at Massah and Meribah. The contrast could not be clearer or more emphatic. In the wilderness, suffering and inconvenience are the signs of an absent or indifferent God, which prompts the question, "Is the Lord with us or not?" In Romans 5, Paul becomes almost rhapsodic on the therapeutic qualities of suffering. "We rejoice in our sufferings," he writes, "knowing that suffering produces endurance, and endurance produces character, and character produces hope, and hope does not disappoint us, because God's love has been poured into our hearts through the Holy Spirit which has been given to us." This view finds an echo in the Epistle of James, where the twelve tribes in the Dispersion to whom the epistle is addressed, are asked immediately after the greeting to "Count it all joy, my brethren, when you meet various trials, for you know that the testing of your faith produces steadfastness. And let steadfastness have its full effect, that you may be perfect and complete, lacking in nothing."

Nothing could be more out of sympathy with the modern temper than these notions that suffering is virtuous and productive of character. We have more in common with the complaining children of Israel in the wilderness than with these sentiments. James L. Crenshaw, writing on suffering in *The Oxford Companion to the Bible*, reminds us of an obvious paradox in suffering. In the first instance, suffering tends to be an isolating phenomenon, separating those who suffer from those who act, and causing the individual to focus upon the suffering either in cause or in consequence, thus promoting what we might call a sense of almost exclusive victimhood. "No one has suffered as I have." The spiritual says it all: "Nobody knows the trouble I've seen, nobody knows but Jesus." In the second instance, however, suffering is community-making, forming a culture of identity among those who share in suffering. One need think only of African Americans and the heritage of slavery; Jews and their history of oppression and of the Holocaust in particular; and in more modern times, a consciousness of group suffering on the part of women and homosexuals, and of others whose point of commonality is that they share in suffering at the hands of others.

How do people of faith deal with suffering, their own and others'? What is the relationship of God to such suffering? These are the hard and pastoral questions with which a doctrine of suffering must deal. One answer is the gnostic one, that since God has nothing to do with suffering, and God is real, therefore suffering is unreal. If one suffers it is either because of some wrong one has done or one's parents have done, which justifies the affliction, or that one is simply not working hard enough or believing hard enough to see through the "illusion" of suffering. Another answer is a form of dualism that suggests that the good God and the evil one have equal force of power, and that one is caught in the tug of war between these titanic forces. This is something of the position of poor old Job, whose loyalty is to be tested through sufferings all too real and vivid. Then there is the view that suffering in this dominion is real and unavoidable, a position clear to any early Christian under persecution, but that in the ultimate dominion to come, under the rule of God, the suffering will be undone, and to have endured will indeed be to have triumphed. This is suffering driven by an eschatological hope, the long run enabling us to endure, and, after a fashion, even to overcome in the short run because of the certain hope of the long run.

If suffering cannot be avoided, as in this world it cannot, it must be given a purpose which makes it bearable as a means to a larger end. In John 16:33, the writer is clear in this point. "In this world ye shall have tribulation." There is no doubt about that. Then Jesus says, "but be of good cheer, I have overcome the world." The implication is clear: those who are with Jesus can do the same thing. Paul many times in his letter speaks of suffering in this short term, the groanings and travails and tribulations, as part of this visible and material world. In 2 Corinthians he speaks of "this slightly momentary affliction" as "preparing for us an eternal weight of glory beyond all comparison." Why? "Because we look not to the things that are seen, but to the things that are unseen; for the things that are seen are transient, but the things that are unseen are eternal." (2 Cor. 4:17-18). It is this passage upon which it can be said that St. Augustine based the entire argument for his great work, *The City of God.*

So the context of suffering is the "eternal weight of glory." The present, while real, is merely present. It is firm confidence in the future that makes the present bearable, and bearing the present well because of that confidence in the eternal yet invisible future produces those qualities of character, those moral characteristics which are stipulated in Romans 5. Suffering for its own sake is not noble, it is masochistic. Suffering, for the Christian, ought to induce both a sense of the past faithfulness when God delivered us through the fiery trials, and a sense of the future hope in which the present trials and sufferings will be vindicated. Those who suffer therefore need to annotate their memories and ignite their hopes. They must not be obsessed by the sufferings of the moment, and they must do all that they can, even in the midst of their very real sufferings, to give glory to God in whose past work and future promise is their only hope. The moral examples of Martin Luther King, Jr., Mahatma Gandhi, Nelson Mandela, and Mother Theresa, among others, remind us of this. It is instructive to note that these examples have seen and known suffering among the despised and neglected of the earth. Sufferings such as they have known is not mere inconvenience. Indeed, as our mothers might have said, the qualities necessary to endure suffering are the very qualities that will help us overcome our suffering.

GOSPEL: JOHN 9:1-41

Suffering takes on a human face in the story of the man born blind and healed by Jesus, as recorded in John 9, the reading appointed for the Gospel in the Lutheran lectionary. Having already discussed John 4:5-42 for the Second Sunday in Lent, the woman at the well, we can devote our attention here to the blind man.

The question the disciples put to Jesus at the beginning of John 9 expresses the assumptions about blindness found in much of Scripture, that it is a punishment or a stigma brought about by some sin. There is no question that the blindness is more than a deformity, more than a disability. It is a punishment. The question of the disciples is, who sinned to merit this punishment of blindness from birth, the man or his parents? The assumption is rooted in Scripture. One need look only at Deuteronomy 28:28, where blindness is listed among the curses, confusions, and frustrations with which God will punish the wicked. Blindness is an imperfection that makes it impossible for a blind man to function as a priest. While one is not to mistreat the blind, and there is a moral obligation to help them, blindness has attached to it at least the suggestion of moral taint.

Jesus does not see it this way, however, at least in this case. Jesus sees the blindness of the man before him as an opportunity to prove the mighty works of God. The blindness may well be of God, but if it is, it is a means to the end of demonstrating the power of God. Within these opening verses of John 9 are introduced the different levels of blindness with which the Scriptures work. Jesus speaks of working while it is day, that is, while there is natural light by which to see. He then goes on to describe himself as the light of the world: "As long as I am in the world, I am the light of the world." This form of light is both illumination and insight, enlightenment and revelation at the same time. To be enlightened is not merely to see, it is to see beyond what appears to be. Such enlightenment is the sort of light or inner sight that allows Paul, in the Romans passage, to look upon the eternal things that are unseen. Such light also gives light to others who may not be enlightened, but who literally walk in the light given them by the enlightened one. All of these meanings and their permutations are available within the first five verses of John 9.

The act of restoring sight to the blind man is an act of creation with striking similarities to the first act of creation by which a living being was made from dust and saliva. Here the blind man is called to life, to a new existence, one he had never before known. To see for the first time is to live, and presumably because he was blind from birth, everything he saw was as new to him as everything that Adam saw was new to him. The blind man is re-made, re-created, and after his bath in the pool of Siloam he is not the man he once was.

This is shocking both to him and to his neighbors, who depended upon the old reality, the fixity of his previous condition as a blind beggar. Consternation overwhelms those who thought they knew him, and hence themselves in relation to him. We may as well surmise that he was equally disoriented by this new condition of his life. After all, he knew how to make a living as a blind beggar. What is he to do now, and how? Not often mentioned in these miracle stories is the risk involved in healing. What happens when the healed one has to adapt to a whole new universe where nothing is as it was? What do those do who care for the sick, when the sick are made well? What do those do whose whole vocation and identity depends upon the condition of their illness, when they are healed? When the stability of suffering is removed, as it was for the children of Israel when they were liberated from slavery in Egypt, often the situation in which the newly liberated one exists is destabilizing, creating profound problems for all concerned.

This is certainly the case here. The blind man is questioned sharply, the integrity of his own experience is challenged, his worthiness to be healed is debated. Indeed, if his blindness was a divine punishment, who was Jesus to undo it? Jesus is subject to sharp criticism for this reason, and the additional one that he performed his act of healing on the sabbath. The parents are interrogated as to their knowledge of the details of their son's blindness and the healing. They feared the Jews, and so said that they should ask the son himself. "He is of age, ask him" (v. 21). When they do, and the blind man repeats the story as he understands it, the critics say, "Give God the praise, this man we know is a sinner." Replying with the only evidence he has, his new sight, the blind man affirms the authenticity of his own experience, his own credential, and disputes carefully with the critics, concluding, "If this man were not from God, he could do nothing." The critics refuse the arguments, the healing, the man, and indeed Jesus, and they cast the formerly blind man out of the community.

It becomes clear that insight among the sighted is a rare and dangerous thing, and the blind who are made to see challenge the moral economy of the community in which they are found. It may be true that in the land of the blind, the one-eyed man is king, but in this case sight and the source of it are too much to risk, and the healed man is expelled. When Jesus says that he came into the world that those who do not see might see, and that those who see might become blind, he uses the paradox as a stick with which to beat those who think they see but who see not. They recognize this by their question, "Are we also blind?" It is their arrogance that maintains their guilt.

Those who see more than others see are a risk to those who think they see all there is to see. The conformity of the group is challenged by those who see beyond the obvious, who see in ways different from the conventional way. Such sight is also called vision, and most communities value vision and visionaries only in hindsight. No community, and no Christian community, willingly follows its visionaries, at least at first. The more established, secure, and comfortable the religious community, the more averse it is to the risk of visionaries and visions that go beyond what everybody else can see at the same time. White Christians in the segregated south of a generation ago had little tolerance for those visionaries in their midst and beyond who preached that God had no use for segregation. Those who held such views either were ignored, or if they persisted, were driven out of the community. Such visions were disturbing to communities that valued order and stability more than they did the truth. Today, hardly any Christian will defend the old segregationist order as approved of God, and few churches, even in the most conservative areas of the country, are organized along the racial lines quite common even twenty-five years ago. The visionaries in their day were not thanked for the disturbing qualities of their vision, although now in retrospect we own them as good and as ours.

John Milton, in his elegaic poem "Lycidas," written to mourn the death of a close clerical friend, describes the pharisaical clergy of the day with the utterly memorable epithet, "blind mouths," referring to their capacity to lead into error by their preaching and teaching. Blindness is not simply a physical malady, a deformity; it is also an inability on the part of those who technically can see, to see beyond what is simply there. The obscuring of vision is a terrible thing, and thus it is a divine thing to make the blind see. It is a healing and heroic act, and next to the resurrection, it is the ultimate miracle. Paul, on the Damascus Road, is blinded; and when the scales drop from his eyes, he who thought he saw everything now saw for the first time. We speak of this as a conversion experience, a turning around, not so much as a second chance but rather as the first time to really get it right. This is the substance of that eternally popular hymn of that old slaver and sinner John Newton, when he writes in "Amazing Grace": "I once was lost, but now am found, was blind, but now I see."

John clearly understands the blind man's condition as an opportunity for God to do a great thing in terms that people can understand. The miracle is not in the act of giving sight to the blind man, although we ought not to disparage that. The miracle is in redefining what it means to see, giving sight, as it were, to those who think they can see. That is the hard part.

The Lutheran readings for this Sunday depart from those discussed above. For example, where Exodus 17 is the portion assigned to the Roman Catholic, Episcopal, and Common Lectionary, the Lutherans take up Isaiah 42:14-21. Now we see why, for verse 16 says, "And I will lead the blind in a way that they know not, in paths that they have not known I will guide them. I will turn the darkness before them into light, the rough places into level ground. These are the things I will do, and I will not forsake them." Here the blind are the ones who need God, and God will provide them with what they need. God does not give them sight. God gives them guidance. What do the blind most require? Security and familiarity as they make their way. They need level ground, no curves or hidden curbs. God will guide them so that they move by faith and not by sight. The figure suggests an intimacy understood only by those who have walked and worked with the blind. There is that gentle equation of dependence and independence, guidance and grace. This is the God who overcomes natural disaster, when at verse 18, God says, "Hear, you deaf, and look, you blind, that you may see," and for whom the greatest blindness is blindness to God's will and way. There are none so blind as those who will not see. It is God's will through his servant to overcome that blindness by leading his people safely through the wilderness.

PSALM 142

Psalm 142 serves the Lutheran liturgy in place of Psalm 95, and the tone is consistent with Isaiah. The psalmist offers this as a lament, a cry for deliverance from personal enemies. "When my spirit is faint"—an acknowledgment of an existential condition—"thou knowest my way," says verse 3. The psalmist needs to know the way out of this condition, but it is hidden, it cannot be readily seen. Persecution is real and on every hand.

Deliverance is sought. Before deliverance arrives, even before this genuine suffering is relieved, the psalmist anticipates the restorative work of the Lord, and vows thanksgiving. At the depths of suffering is the confidence in ultimate delivery. The suffering is real, and so too is the promise of delivery.

SECOND LESSON: EPHESIANS 5:8-14

In Ephesians 5:8-14, the familiar theme of light and darkness is again developed. This has become the organizing metaphor for the Lutheran readings on this Sunday. The faithful are themselves "light in the Lord," and are bidden to "walk as children of light." The works of darkness are unfruitful, and Christians are to shine light upon the darkness to expose wickedness. The gift of the resurrection is light, being visible to God and the world: "Awake, O sleeper, and arise from the dead, and Christ shall give you light." We sleep at night and in darkness, unawake, unaware, invisible. We are as the dead. To wake is to live in the light and to be the light. This light is not mere wisdom or insight, or an illumination. This is exemplary light, light by which others as well. This light is not unlike the light of which Jesus speaks when he says, "Let your light so shine before others that they may see your good works and glorify your father which is in heaven." There is introduced here the disturbing notion that somebody else's vision may in fact depend upon yours. Your example has an evangelistic effect for good or ill, and ideally for good. Your good works are not for yourself, not even for God, but for the edification of others. That painful implication for the character of our own conduct, and the content of our character, cannot be evaded. It is an essential ingredient to discipleship.

Prayer for the Preacher Preparing for the Third Sunday in Lent

O God, who art the restorer of the fallen, and the lover of innocence: direct towards thyself the hearts of thy people; that they, whom thou has delivered from the darkness of unbelief, may not depart from the light of thy truth; through Jesus Christ our Lord, Amen. (Gelasian Prayers, p. 86).

Fourth Sunday in Lent

Lectionary	First Lesson	Psalm	Second Lesson	Gospel
Episcopal	I Sam. 16:1-13	Psalm 23	Eph. 5:(1-7) 8-14	John 9:1-13 (14-27), 28-38
Roman Catholic	I Sam. 16:1b, 6-7, 10-13	Ps. 23:1-6	Eph. 5:8-14	John 9:1-41 *or* 9:1, 6-9, 13-17, 34-38
Revised Common	I Sam. 16:1-13	Psalm 23	Eph. 5:8-14	John 9:1-41
Lutheran	Hosea 5:15—6:2	Psalm 43	Rom. 8:1-10	Matt. 20:17-28

FIRST LESSON: I SAMUEL 16:1-13

Once upon a time, before the current episodes of liturgical renewal, the Fourth Sunday in Lent had a clear and unique personality and provided a welcome respite from the rigors of Lent, and a bright hint of things to come. Its Latin title was *Dominica Refectionis*, from the Gospel text of that day, which was the account of our Lord's feeding of the five thousand. The Roman Church called the Fourth Sunday in Lent *Laetare* Sunday from the first word of the Collect for the day, which was "Rejoice ye with Jerusalem, and be glad with her, all ye that love her." Refreshment Sunday was like water from the rock, a refreshment to pilgrims in the wilderness on their way to the promises. In England, mid-Lent Sunday came to be known as Mothering Sunday, and on that day special devotion was made to the Mother of God, pilgrimages were made to the Mother Church, or Cathedral of the diocese, and indentured servants were permitted to visit their mothers, and often did so with presents of poppy-seed cakes known as *simnel* cakes. Where flowers had been prohibited on the altars for Lent, they were returned on this Sunday as a harbinger of the festival to come. The first lesson at Matins on this Sunday in ancient times was taken from Genesis 43, where Joseph, taken as a type of Christ, refreshes his brethren in the midst of their famine.

In certain traditions some of these customs and associations for the Fourth Sunday in Lent are invoked, but the lessons no longer affirm the theme of refreshment. There is some advantage, however, in keeping alive the notion of mid-Lent as a time for pause and renewal of the people in their Lenten ambitions. Ash Wednesday seems a long time ago, and Easter seems equally distant, and all the more so with an impatient people and the short attention span of our modern, fast-moving culture. Many will be spiritually tired and frustrated by their inability to do all that they had hoped and intended. Mid-Lent may well present a pastoral opportunity to teach the faithful that they cannot on their own do everything all of the time. The salutary themes of the old Refreshment Sunday can be retained or invoked with appropriate adaptations, while continuing in the teaching that the modern lectionaries provide for this Sunday.

Reserving comment on the Lutheran lections for later, it should be noted that the Roman Catholic, Episcopal, and Common Lectionary share all of the lessons for this Sunday. The first lesson is the account of the calling of David, and the prophet Samuel's mission amongst the sons of Jesse. The first theme of which we need take note is that of rejection. God has rejected Saul. God had commanded Saul to destroy Agag and the Amalekites and all of their goods, but Saul had spared Agag and the best of the animals and all that was good. He would not destroy them utterly, and thus Saul disobeyed God and incurred the divine wrath. Samuel, while sympathetic to Saul, informed the king of the divine displeasure and made it clear to Saul that "to obey is better than sacrifice . . . for rebellion is as the sin of divinization, and stubbornness is as iniquity. Because you have rejected the word of the Lord," says Samuel to Saul at 1 Samuel 15:23, "he has rejected you from being king."

This may seem a harsh judgement on Saul's exercise of mercy. He used his own judgment in interpreting the divine command, and God regarded this not as a judgment in the field, but as rank disobedience, and from that time onward could not trust Saul to do as he was told. Saul had ceased to enjoy the confidence of his Commander-in-Chief, and a new king who would be faithful and obedient was to be found. This is the commission given to Samuel at the beginning of Genesis 16. The context is a sad one. Saul is rejected, God is disappointed, and Samuel, grieving over Saul, is sent out to find the king's successor among the sons of Jesse. It should be noted that Samuel was asked to finish the job that Saul had botched, and at 1 Samuel 15:33, having sent for Agag, whom Saul had spared, Samuel "hewed Agag in pieces before the Lord in Gilgal." It will be difficult to find much good news here. The lesson is clear, if somewhat unpalatable: God's commands are to be obeyed. Mercy is not to be found in 1 Samuel 15.

The second theme that presents itself here is choice, for it is Samuel's commission to choose as Saul's successor one of the sons of Jesse. The standard of choice is the standard of conformity to God's will. Having chosen the wrong man in Saul, God intends to get it right this time. Jesse is apprehensive of the purpose of Samuel's visit, and wishes to make certain that the Judge comes peaceably: once he is reassured, the father summons seven of his sons to pass in review before the scrutiny of Samuel and of God. It is clear that Samuel might have chosen any one of them, and particularly the attractive Eliab; but God is not so easily impressed and warns Samuel: "Do not look on his appearance or on the height of his stature, because I have rejected him; for the Lord sees not as man sees; man looks on the outward appearance, but the Lord looks on the heart" (1 Samuel 16:7).

Not one of those sons of Jesse would do, and so the youngest one, absent from the review, is sent for. David is thus summoned to stand before Samuel, and we learn that to the outward eye he was "ruddy, and had beautiful eyes, and was handsome" (1 Sam. 16:12). The Lord was pleased, and ordered that David should be anointed: "Arise, anoint him; for this is he" (1 Sam. 16:12). And from that day onward the spirit of the Lord came mightily upon David. As he was no less handsome than his brother Eliab, against whom God had warned on the basis of mere appearance, we must infer that in addition to his outward comeliness David had a disposition of the heart that was pleasing to God.

The character of David is complex, and that complexity should not be minimalized. Christians tend to idealize David as the ancestor of our Lord, and therefore often find it difficult to account for the complex human character that allows David to be at once the apple of God's eye and the great sinner against God. How do we reconcile the heroic slayer of Goliath and the sweet singer of psalms with the conniving adulterer and murderer of Uriah, his mistress's husband? Was there war raging within him between his good and his bad natures? Are we able to forgive the bad in light of the great good? How do we understand David's relationship with Saul, with Bathsheba, with Uriah, and with Jonathan? Surely David is no one-dimensional figure. His complexity and his intense humanity must be taken into account. His life is summarized in 1 Kings 15:5, where it says of him that he did "right in the eyes of the Lord, and turned not aside . . . all the days of his life, save only in the matter of Uriah the Hittite."

PSALM 23

The promise of God's choice among the sons of Jesse is amply fulfilled, and all of Israel's future hopes trace their descent from David, so much so that the messianic designation becomes "son of David." In the New Testament and in the patristic commentaries, David is a type of Christ. For example, his exorcism of the evil spirit that was in Saul is understood as a prefiguration of Christ's triumph over Satan. His persecution at the hands of Saul prefigures Christ's at the hands of Herod. Still, the stumbling block of his abominable sin with Bathsheba must be addressed. Augustine regards his moral crimes as temporary, though flagrant, lapses, thus allowing David to become a model of penitence and of God's grace. He thus becomes a guide to spiritual reformation and repentance, and the penitential psalms attributed to him, especially Psalm 51, become a penitential manual for the faithful. The argument is this: if God could forgive so flagrant a sinner as David, then no one should be without hope. His sin is an opportunity for God's grace and mercy.

The claims upon David are many. For some he is the exemplar of what the nineteenth-century American Protestants liked to call "muscular Christianity," a man's man, a military genius, a wise lawgiver, or a politician who did what had to be done. Others see in him an aesthete, a poet, and musician not dissimilar to the pagan Orpheus. Still others see in him a man of passion who loved Bathsheba, his friend's wife, and Jonathan, his king's son. None of these alone is David, but David is not complete without all aspects of these, which add to his immense human complexity and appeal. To think of him merely as the youthful giant-killer and composer of psalms is to miss what the writers of the books of Samuel, Kings, and Chronicles are at such pains to present to us. The tensions apparent in this heroic life are never resolved. David is an untidy figure, not easily summarized. Perhaps it is this human complexity on an enormous scale, worthy of, say, Shakespeare, that makes him a figure of enduring interest and significance to us.

The problem with Psalm 23 is that we think we know all that we need to know about it. It will be difficult to sustain the attention of the congregation, and even of the preacher, in a text which is so fundamental a part of our piety that it may be said to be the one universal piece of Scripture known even to the godless. For many, Psalm 23 is the first bit of Scripture that we learn. For even more it is the last we hear at death's door and at the grave itself. What dare we make of it between our beginning and our end? That is the question the preacher confronts when Psalm 23 is invited into the liturgy as it is today. "Is it possible," in the words of my old teacher and colleague, Krister Stendahl, "to redeem the familiar?"

At the risk of a charge of "deconstructionism," let me suggest that we should substitute a sense of comfort for one of consolation. The twenty-third Psalm is a source of enormous consolation. The phrase, "Yea, though I walk through the valley of the shadow of death, I will fear no evil," contributes much to the therapeutic nature of this psalm. This is why it features in the burial office and at the bedside of the fearful and of the dying. The structure of the psalm, however, has more to say about strength-giving, for that is what comfort is, than about consolation or resignation to imponderable and implacable circumstances. Because the Lord is my shepherd, as the Coverdale translation renders, "therefore I lack nothing." Since my shepherd, unlike any other shepherd, is the Lord, my needs are met. Often we read this as saying that the shepherd belongs to me, the Lord is "my" shepherd, but the sense is different when we read it this way, "because I belong to the Lord," therefore I shall want for nothing.

Everything I require, including the capacity to cope with those things beyond my capacity, is provided by the Lord. The psalm opens and concludes on that affirmation. My strength comes from the fact that goodness and mercy do follow me all the days of my life, and I dwell in God's house forever. In other words, I have been enabled to get to where I am heading because I am guided and protected by one who will not let me stray. I am enabled, in the language of the day, not just protected, but enabled to gain the pasturage I require. I cannot do it on my own: my shepherd enables me to do what I must do and to go where I must go, even through the valley of the shadow of death.

The psalm speaks of the experience of the faithful, wisely led. The faithful have the experience of green pastures, still waters, and the paths of righteousness. These paths of righteousness take us from the dimension of safety and provision into the moral way. He leads me into the right way, we are led in ways of discernment, even judgment. Given such discernment, and the strengthening presence of the one who gives it, even the valley of the shadow of death is not fearsome, "for thou art with me."

We are enabled to deal with the greatest of life's fears, the fear of death. If we can cope with this, what else is there to fear? Read carefully, we know that the passage and the good shepherd do not spare us death, we are not given immunity or immortality. It does not spare us even proximity to death. The valley of the shadow of death is that low place over which death hovers, obscuring the light, making us aware of the presence of death and of the fragility of light and life. One senses this great brooding mountain that casts a shadow over the valley through which one must go. It is darkness at noon, but one must pass through in order to get to the other side. It is not death that is to be overcome here. It is the fear of the presence of death, and the valley of the shadow is in many respects far more frightening than death itself. Even fear is not overcome. Fear is not dismissed but we are not left alone with fear. Alone in the valley of the shadow we might very well perish of fright if of nothing else. But we are not alone in such a ghostly place. Why? "For thou art with me, thy rod and thy staff they comfort me."

What are the other places of fear and anxiety? The presence of our enemies, those who hate us, some with cause, others without any cause. It is a fearful thing to be in the presence of one's enemies, yet even in such a place of fear we have nothing to fear. Hospitality drives out fear, the table makes partakers of enemies: "Thou preparest a table before me in the presence of mine enemies." There is nothing more intimate than a shared meal. So great is the sense of relief and joy in the Psalm that the final verse turns into a doxology of praise and affirmation. Awareness of such providence leads only and always to praise. This is the sense of Henry

Baker's paraphrase of Psalm 23, in his nineteeth-century hymn, "The King of Love My Shepherd Is," when at the last stanza he says:

> And so through all the length of days
> Thy goodness faileth never:
> Good Shepherd, may I sing thy praise
> Within thy house forever.

The twenty-third Psalm and the ancient theme of refreshment on the Fourth Sunday in Lent are compatible in a wonderful way. It is the *good* shepherd, as opposed to the calloused or indifferent one, who provides nourishment and refreshment for the flock. The patristic commentators saw in Psalm 23 a type of eucharist, a meal of renewal and refreshment. Henry Baker's paraphrase iterates that sense when, in a stanza often omitted from his hymn in more "low church" traditions, he says of stanza 5:

> Thou spread'st a table in my sight;
> Thy unction grace bestoweth:
> And oh, what transport of delight
> From thy pure chalice floweth!

The themes of guidance, confidence, hope, and praise are found also in Psalm 43, which the Lutherans read today. The vindication of the righteous against the wicked is called for, and God is asked to support the righteous in the cause. Help in time of need is begged. The oppression of the enemy is real and the question is, Why does God seem so far away? Yet the very God whose apparent absence is decried is the God to whom praise on the lyre is to be offered for deliverance. Hope overcomes the disquieted soul, hope in God is the only answer, even in the midst of troubles, for God is my hope and my help.

SECOND LESSON: ROMANS 8:1-10

On the Third Sunday in Lent we discussed Ephesians 5:8-14, which was then the Lutheran lection and is now the reading for the Roman Catholic, Episcopal, and the Common Lectionary. Today's Lutheran epistle is Romans 8:1-10. Paul is eager for the faithful to appreciate the difference between life in Christ and life in bondage to sin and death. To those who are in Christ there is no condemnation. The commentaries remind us that condemnation means irreversible doom, indeed, death. Sin itself has been condemned to death, and those in Christ are freed from the domination of the law of sin and death. This freedom was not possible under the law, but through the incarnation of our Lord the just requirements of the law are fulfilled. There is therefore a new standard of conduct and expectation, and that is the law of the spirit. Paul sets up one of his familiar comparisons, this time between the spirit and the flesh. Elsewhere the comparison is between the visible and the invisible, or the transient and the permanent. Here it is the spiritual that is opposed to the material. Those who submit themselves to the spiritual, that is, those who are prepared to live in the spirit, are freed from the demands of the material.

This is a new order that turns the world upside down, the paradox of Christian living where what you see is neither what you get nor what you should want. The material world seduces and frustrates, and it holds its adherents captive to those tangible but transitory pleasures that the world affords. To be materially minded is to not simply like the things of this world and life, but to be seduced into thinking that they are the only things that count, the only things that are "really real." Those who are spiritually minded, however, do not live out of the world, but they are not under the dominion of the world. No prison can capture such a spirit-minded person, and no worldly "success" can satisfy such a spiritually minded person. Materially minded people are hostile to God because God seems inferior to the more material and amenable gods of the world. Such people cannot submit themselves and their desires to God. They are in fact hostile to God, and they cannot please God. The apparent "freedom" of the materially minded is really slavery, a bondage to sensation and to that which can be demonstrated and quantified and possessed.

They are to be compared with the Christians who are not in the flesh but in the spirit, and who therefore are to submit to a higher law that frees them from the devices and desires of the flesh. All of this is the result of the new order introduced by Christ, and for which one need not wait for the eschaton. This point is important for believers of both then and now. The new life, the life of the spirit, has already come. It has been introduced by the resurrection and is not to be postponed to an indefinite future. This is not a counsel to wait for the good future. The good future is here and now, and the faithful in Christ who truly are in the spirit will recognize this and live accordingly. The rule of the law and the flesh has been abrogated. We do not have to wait. We are no longer in the flesh. We are in the spirit. Tense is important. It does not say that you will be in the spirit, it announces as a present fact, an accomplishment before our eyes, that we are in the spirit. The immediate implication is a liberated life in the face of whatever the worst is that the world can do. To those who think themselves victims of circumstance, Christ has changed the circumstances. We already have that for which we aspire. Just as the psalmist in Psalm 43 cries out in doubt and fear for that which he already has, so too the faithful in the spirit already have that which is essential to life, a life pleasing to God and *contra mundum*, against the world.

GOSPEL: MATTHEW 20:17-28

The healing of the blind man was the Gospel lesson for the Third Sunday in Lent, and is treated there. Here we will discuss Matthew 20:17-28, the Gospel in the Lutheran lectionary for this Sunday.

The verse in Matthew 20 immediately preceding today's reading is the famous reversal saying of Jesus in which he declares, "So the last will be first and the first, last." It therefore comes as something of a shock when we find, a few verses along, the mother of the sons of Zebedee asking for preferment for her sons. "Command that these two sons of mine may sit, one at your right hand, one at your left, in your kingdom" (Matt. 20:21). She just doesn't get it. By this construction of the text she looks badly, a pushy mother eager for her sons to make their way in the coming establishment of Jesus. In the parallel passage in Mark, the apostles make their own requests. In Matthew they look less badly, but at the expense of their mother. They don't get it either. The kingdom of which Jesus speaks is not one with a worldly pecking order. It is not one that merely maintains the same world order but with a different cast of characters, like some Latin American political revolution; it is a new order where the focus is upon service and not on lordly power. The movement in this passage is from a statement of the sacrificial mission of Christ and his forthcoming passion, death, and resurrection (vv. 12-19); through the confusion of that ultimate destiny with the ambition of the disciples to a place of future glory (vv. 20-23); and the statement of risk and expectation by which an ethic of service and sacrifice is to be the defining characteristic of the coming kingdom.

In the middle of the second section is the question Jesus puts to the disciples, "Are you able to drink the cup that I drink?" And the all-too-ready answer of the disciples, "We are able." There is an understandable eagerness here, and what is wrong with spiritual ambition? Nothing is wrong with spiritual ambition except in its capacity to divert the spiritually ambitious from the cost of discipleship. All seek preferment in the kingdom. The very notion of preferment is contrary to the nature of the kingdom itself, however, and that fact is often forgotten or overlooked by the spiritually ambitious. Of all the forms of pride, and spiritual ambition is just one such form, spiritual pride is perhaps the worst, for it takes earthly things, transient and material as they are, and elevates them to the primacy of the spiritual. That is a form of idolatry and blindness to which religious people are particularly prone. It should be noted that all of the people who take part in this passage are religious people, the good people, the church people, the intimate followers of the Lord. Even they are not immune to this insidious temptation. Jesus makes emphatic the radical content of the gospel. Not only will the first be last and the last, first, but the very nature of being first is now subject to change. He or she who would rule must become the servant of all. For those used to being spiritually first, this will be the hardest cross to bear.

Prayer for the Preacher Preparing for the Fourth Sunday in Lent

O God, merciful and everlasting, who didst not spare thine own son, but gavest him up for us all, that he, the true bread of life, might feed and refresh us: grant, we beseech thee, that we may receive him gladly and thus be strengthened in every peril and saved to all eternity, through the same Jesus Christ, our Lord. Amen.

Fifth Sunday in Lent

Lectionary	First Lesson	Psalm	Second Lesson	Gospel
Episcopal	Ezek. 37:1-3 (4-10), 11-14	Psalm 130	Rom. 6:16-23	John 11:(1-17), 18-44
Roman Catholic	Ezek. 37:12-14	Ps. 130:1-8	Rom. 8:8-11	John 11:1-45 or 11:3-7, 17, 20-27, 33-45
Revised Common	Ezek. 37:1-14	Psalm 130	Rom. 8:6-11	John 11:1-45
Lutheran	Ezek. 37:1-3 (4-10), 11-14	Ps. 116:1-8	Rom. 8:11-19	John 11:1-53 or 11:47-53

FIRST LESSON: EZEKIEL 37:1-14

This Sunday was from ancient times called Passion Sunday, for on it began the shift in attention from the Lenten pilgrimage of the faithful and their instruction in the faith, to an ever-increasing focus upon our Lord and preparations for the consideration of the solemnities of Holy Week. It was customary to place purple veils over crosses and crucifixes, and this for many marked the beginning of "high Lent," or what was called "Passiontide," a season of intense focus upon the cross. The veiling of the cross is an interesting custom. To us, such an act seems one of reverence or of mourning, hiding the crucified one until Easter day. To the ancients, however, the cross was a symbol of victory and glory. It was veiled not so much to mourn, but to lend emphasis to the fact that the victory of which the cross was the symbol was not yet achieved. Some of the earliest crosses were decorated with gems and precious stones, and were set, especially in the Eastern Church, within a crown, very much like the cross and crown pins once popular as medals for perfect attendance in Sunday School. Such a display of splendor seemed inappropriate at Passiontide, and so the symbol of victory was veiled until Easter. The very act of veiling, however, added emphasis to the cross and indicated that the liturgical season, on the Fifth Sunday in Lent, had taken a decided turn. The veil was not unlike the veil over Moses' face when he descended from the mountain, which he wore not as a matter of modesty but to protect the people from the terrible glare of a face that had been in proximity to God. The paradox of the Passion, and of this Sunday which once bore that title, is that even as we are called to contemplate the cross and to face it squarely, to consider once again the drama of our redemption, it is too much for us, too bright, we cannot bear to see what we must see. The veil is not a bow to modesty. It is of necessity, to protect the frailty of our own hearts.

Contemporary liturgical usage has done away with the distinctive character of the Fifth Sunday in Lent, and the Sixth Sunday, commonly called

Palm Sunday, is now properly the Sunday of the Passion and the first day of Holy Week or the Week of the Passion. The Fifth Sunday in Lent, however, retains its function as a transition Sunday from one Lenten mood or mode to another, and in the orchestration of the keeping of Lent, the benefits of such a transition should be utilized. The shift in focus from self to Christ on this occasion is a salutary corrective to the tendency to self-obsession during Lent. If one is not careful Lent can become something of a liturgical twelve-step program in self-improvement for the faithful, a combination of a diet and exercise regimen with a built-in cure for personal bad habits. Losing weight or taking exercise, or curbing one's appetite for sweets or drink become ends in and of themselves, and thus are just one more scheme at self-perfection. I have tried, in my own liturgical observance, to guide my parishioners into consciousness of the Fifth Sunday in Lent's hinge purpose by suggesting that our moral energy shift from considerations of our self to considerations of our Savior. After all, the Lenten disciplines, the acts of abstinence, of self-discipline, and charity are not goals in themselves but are designed to make it easier for us, now less distracted by the demands of the world, to come closer to thinking of Christ. Lent is not for self-improvement. Lent is to better equip the self to consider holy things. If we have done well what we set out to do, by now we should be somewhat better prepared to contemplate the realities of the Passion, and the intense spiritual demands that will take us to Holy Week and to the foot of the cross on Good Friday.

All of the lessons today help us face mighty things, and they are all, as it were, in anticipation of the great days and themes ahead. The powerful image of the valley of the dry bones is the common Old Testament lesson for all of the lectionaries today, and there are few more vivid and demanding images in all of Scripture. The spectre of a vast valley filled with the dry bones of the dead is itself a terrifying figure. The scale of death and uselessness is enormous. We do not know how these dead came to be dead. It could have been from famine, pestilence, plague, or warfare. In the nuclear age the image of such vast and complete devastation is, alas, not beyond our power to imagine. How death in the valley came about, however, we do not know. That death did come about, and in a mighty, final, and terrifying way, is unambiguously clear. The text sets the prophet down in the midst of these bones and emphasizes the fact that they are very dry. This is so that we do not lose the sense of real and devastating death. These dead are really dead, and have been for some time. Their bones are bleached, and no hint of life clings to them. They are their own memorial to some past epic tragedy or disaster. There can be no life here.

The Lord asks the prophet the question of the day: "Son of man, can these bones live?" And the prophet replies prudently, "O Lord God, thou knowest." The Lord then instructs the prophet to prophesy to the bones, informing them of God's intention for them, that they should be reconstituted and live. The prophet obeys, and with a rattling noise the bones knit themselves into human form and are covered with skin. They have all of their former properties save the breath of life. The prophet is instructed to prophesy to the breath. The breath is summoned from the four winds to give life to these slain, and it is so, "and they lived, and stood upon their feet, an exceeding great host" (Ezek. 37:10).

The vision of the bleached bones is exceeded only by the vision of the reconstituted army into whom the breath of life has been breathed. They stand in serried rank assembled just as they were before their slaughter. What can such a thing mean? It is the Lord who proceeds to explain his own miracle to the prophet, who throughout this episode is an instrumental witness to the mighty workings of the Lord. The bones are Judah and Samaria, defeated in fact and in spirit. They believe that it is all over for them, and that they can never live again. "Our bones are dried up, and our hope is cut off: we are clean cut off." The kingdom of Israel is lost. The chances of restoring the kingdom, and the glory of the kingdom, are about as great as the resuscitation of an army of corpses. It is the purpose of the Lord, through the instrumentality of the prophet, to counter such defeatism, and by the remarkable agency of raising to life a slain army, to demonstrate that the people's hopes are not cut off. The reason these hopes are not cut off is because the Lord is still powerful. When the Lord opens the graves of the dead and by the power of his spirit puts new life into the dead, then not only will they live, but they will know that the Lord lives as well. It is put into the mouth of the prophet to say these things: "And I will put my Spirit within you, and you shall live, and I will place you in your own land; then you shall know that I, the Lord, have spoken, and I have done it, says the Lord" (Ezek. 37:14).

By the Lord's own interpretation of the vision, from verse 11 through to the end of verse 14, the vision is understood to be an allegory of the restoration to its own land of defeated and defeatist Israel. It is God's account of the regeneration, indeed the resurrection, of a whole people, and their hopes with them. The purpose of this regeneration, however, is not merely philanthropic. It is also to show the glory and the power of the Lord. It is the demonstration of divine majesty and power, not a fluke of nature or an act of charity, that should command our attention here.

An interesting characteristic of this passage is the Lord's tutorial of his own prophet. It is the Lord who sets the prophet in the midst of the valley. It is the Lord who asks the question, "Son of man, can these bones live?" and gives the answers and their interpretation. The prophet is something of a straight man to the Lord, who uses him to make his several points.

It is the Lord who tells the prophet what to say. And it is the Lord who tells the prophet his own divine intention. The prophet's job is not to get in the way of the mighty workings of God, but to proclaim those workings to the people of God.

It is also important here to note that the Lord has concerned himself with a dispirited people, people who have lost their will and their nerve, and who are as good as dead. He addresses the discouraged, the down-hearted, the depressed. Here is a case where things are better than they appear to be. The appearance is of wholesale death and destruction. Any sensible person would take note of that. "Who are we in the face of such calamity? We are no better than these who are dead and bleached." Even the prophet, who is presumably intimate with God, at least initially concedes the overwhelming "reality" of the situation. His answer to the divine question, "Son of man, can these bones live?" is at best coy and evasive: "Thou knowest, Lord." His real and hidden answer is probably "No," but he is shrewd enough to recognize a divine rhetorical question when he hears one.

This text has long been a favorite in the African American religious community, and the reason is not too difficult to discern. A decimated people who may well have lost faith in themselves and have come to believe in the inevitability of their destruction, who have come to believe their oppressors' opinion of themselves, are a people as good as dead. Yet it is the will of God for the glory of God that they should live, and, overcoming the odds of their own sense of defeat and loss, become a community of the resurrection. God's allegory of the house of Israel recalled to life and purpose in the face of calamitous defeat, is an allegory capable of giving life to any people whose God is the Lord. It is not for just any people that this can happen. It can happen only to those whose God is the Lord. The object of the enterprise is to show the power of God, and thus faithfulness to God is the necessary context for such an extraordinary demonstration of the power of God. It is not merely nature that is reversed, or adversity that is overcome. It is the absolute power of the Lord who alone can create life and make the dead live again. This is the ultimate claim and work of God.

PSALM 130

Psalm 130 is a lyrical expression of confidence in the midst of depression, and its opening words: "Out of the depths I cry to thee, O Lord," places us with the psalmist at the darkest part of the valley of the shadow. The psalm addresses the fundamental problem of the faithful. How does one maintain one's hope and faith in the midst of defeat and despair? How is one reconciled to the fact that most of us spend far more of our time in the depths than we do exalted in the heights? How do we deal with a reality in which the negative is more normative than the positive? Put another way by that domestic prophet, Erma Bombeck: "If life is a bowl of cherries, why am I always in the pits?"

Somehow we have come to buy a version of religious faith that says that despair and depression are abnormal. The faithful, so we assume, are always upbeat, happy, productive, and living examples of the life to come. When adversity comes their way, these faithful deal with it heroically and graciously. They never cry out. They never doubt God or themselves. These are the ones upon whom the rest of us depend. At its worst, this version of "faithful living" says that if there is something wrong, there is something wrong with you. Of course, this version fails to take into account that indeed there is something wrong with us, all of us, and fundamentally wrong, and that is why there is something wrong. Our knowledge is imperfect, and so too is our vision. As Paul said, things are so bad that we do not even know how to pray for relief. Most of us in our heart of hearts acknowledge the fact that we live most of our lives in the depths, quiet lives of desperation, longing to make sense and connections but never being quite able to do so. We construct elaborate diversions to make life in the depths bearable, habitable. Illusions are never more valuable than in the depths. Every once in a while, however, every once in a while reality breaks through and we see where and who and what we really are.

To speak of despair and the depths is not necessarily to speak of clinical depression. The depths of which the psalmist speaks are somehow less exotic and more fundamental than that. The closest condition to it, I suggest, is what we today call anxiety. Woody Allen may well, in his heyday, have been the apostle of anxiety chic. In his parody of a commencement cliché, Allen once said: "More than at any time in our history, mankind faces a crossroad. One path leads to despair and utter hopelessness, the other to total extinction. Let us pray we have the wisdom to choose correctly." That sounds like the choice of the valley of the dry bones. If Woody Allen is too flippant, perhaps we can take more seriously the words of the German theologian, Helmut Thielicke, who in his small book of sermons, *The Silence of God*, defines the depths as neither fear nor fear of death, but rather as anxiety, that mid-twentieth-century social disease. "Anxiety," he says, "is the secret world of modern man." Citing poll data then contemporary with his writing but now forty years old, Thielicke observes that most modern university students identified anxiety as their greatest emotional concern. Those of us who deal with those students, now late middle-aged adults, and with their children and grandchildren, know that the poll is not out of date at all. Anxiety is the common denominator that binds all our people together in a bundle of anxieties, living daily in the depths. It was the late Rollo May who coined the phrase the "age of anxiety," noting that until fairly recent times anxiety was not something about which emotionally stable people liked to speak. Modernity, however, has taught us that there is much about which to be anxious. Charlotte Elliott, in her hymn "Just as I Am," knows the "age of anxiety" though she lived from 1789 to 1871, and in the third stanza of her hymn, describes the anxious one:

> *Just as I am, though toss'd about*
> *With many a conflict, many a doubt,*
> *Fightings and fears within, without,*
> *O Lamb of God, I come.*

The psalmist with brutal honesty acknowledges the reality of the depths. The sense of anxiety about life itself is palpable: "fighting and fears, within, without." The depths are real. They are not to be minimalized. They are not to be dismissed with cheap cheer and cheaper grace. Martin Luther's paraphrase of Psalm 130 is found in the first three hymnals of the German Reformation. Translated in 1863 into English, by Catherine Winkworth, its four stanzas take us through the mood swings of the Psalms. "Out of the depths I cry to thee." This is the place where the psalmist is. He asks not for justice, but for mercy: "If thou rememberest each misdeed, if each should have its rightful meed, who may abide his presence?" The answer is, no one. And so the final stanza of Luther's paraphrase reads:

> *Though great our sins and sore our woes,*
> *His grace much more aboundeth;*
> *His helping love no limit knows,*
> *Our utmost need it soundeth.*
> *Our kind and faithful shepherd, he,*
> *Who shall at last set Israel free*
> *From all their sin and sorrow.*

It is this sense of the abounding grace of the kind and faithful shepherd to which Thielicke refers when he says, speaking again of anxiety, that "anxiety is a broken bond and love is the bond restored." The restoration of that bond is the basis of the hope in stanza 7, "O Israel, hope in the Lord, for with the Lord there is steadfast love, and with him is plenteous redemption." Once that bond is acknowledged as broken, hence the reality of the depths, and once one calls to the God whose property it is to restore that bond, and who does so out of love for us greater than our love for ourselves or for God, then the work of redemption has begun, and in words

alien to the psalmist, but of more than usual pertinence to us, nothing and
no one can separate us from the love of God. This is what St. Paul means
in Romans 8, when he writes, "Who shall separate us from the love of
Christ? Shall tribulation or distress or persecution or famine or nakedness
or peril or sword?" To this list we might add depression, anxiety, fear,
and failure—and we know his answer. In fact it may be said, for homiletical
and pastoral purposes at least, that Romans 8 is an answer to Psalm 130.
"Nay, in all these things we are more than conquerors through him that
loved us." Then, in what may arguably be the most compelling prose in
the entire New Testament, including John 3:16, Paul concludes Romans
8: "For I am persuaded that neither death, nor life, nor angels, nor prin-
cipalities, nor things present, nor things to come, nor powers, nor height,
nor depth, nor any other creature will be able to separate us from the love
of God which is in Christ Jesus our Lord." The depths are real. So too
are the heights.

SECOND LESSON: ROMANS 8:8-23

All of the New Testament epistle readings come from Romans 8, but none
takes us through to the triumphant end of the chapter to which I have above
referred. The Roman Catholics and the Common Lectionary read from
verse 8 to verse 11. The Lutherans take it from verses 11 through 19, and
the Episcopalians read from verse 16 through verse 23. The preacher who
reads only those portions of Romans 8 for which his or her lectionary calls
does a terrible disservice to the chapter and to the listeners, for Romans
8 is one of the most tightly argued chapters in Paul's most tightly argued
letter. We begin where we left off last Sunday. The context of the chapter
is God's saving and transforming act in Christ, by which all of the things
we might assume about the domination of the world by sin, the flesh, and
the devil, are put under submission, their tyranny broken, and the goal of
a reconciled and permanent fellowship with God achieved beyond all limits.
It is that fact which the last verses of the chapter celebrate and affirm, in
short, the answer to the despair of Psalm 130. The discussion of Romans
8:1-10 we took up last Sunday in the Lutheran lectionary. Today, in the
pericope assigned to the Lutherans, vv. 11-19, we find Paul speaking of
the claims of the spirit over those of the flesh. Those who live by the flesh
die by the flesh. Debtors to the flesh inherit only what flesh is capable of
delivering, death and dry bones. The deeds of the body, while they may
seem important and even permanent, are not. They are subject to the rule
of death. The dry bones were once flesh and blood, living beings. When
the spirit departed from them, however, their flesh was nothing, and they
were dead and dried up. They came to life only when the breath of the

spirit of God was poured back into them. To live according to the flesh is to inherit the inevitable end of death. God, though, has seen fit to give us an inheritance of the spirit that transcends the life of flesh and death. This inheritance will free us from bondage, slavery to the power of the flesh, the pervasive influence of the body, and the inevitable reign of death. Those who are heirs of God, sons of God—that is, those capable of inheriting— are led or enabled by the spirit. Their inheritance is the Spirit, which makes them intimate with God. Hence they address God intimately, familiarly. We are told by modern commentators that "Abba, Father," at verse 15, can be translated as "Daddy," a term of endearment which emphasizes the benevolent aspect of the relationship of heirs: as the old theological for-mulation puts it, "children by adoption and grace" who are destined to inherit all of the best the father has to offer. The spirit confirms the legitimacy of the heirs at verse 16: "It is the Spirit himself bearing witness with our spirit that we are children of God." Our identity as heirs of God, and fellow or "joint heirs" with Christ, depends upon our capacity to suffer with him in order that we may also be glorified with him (v. 17).

Paul then turns to the subject of suffering. Again, it is not metaphorical or symbolical suffering, but real. We have an idea as to the nature of the sufferings to which he directs his Roman listeners, when from verse 35 to the end of the chapter he specifies what they are: charges against God's elect, separation from Christ, tribulation, distress, famine, nakedness, peril, and sword. "For thy sake we are being killed all the day long; we are regarded as sheep to be slaughtered." No. This is not mere anxiety. This is not merely a crisis of belief or of identity. These sufferings, by the standard of the world, have the capacity to destroy everything the world values.

These sufferings, returning to the pericope, Paul says are not worth comparing with the glory that is to be revealed to us. It almost sounds like the adage "no pain, no gain," and it is that, and so very much more. The creation is not yet ready for the revealing of the heirs of God. At the moment, for the time being, things are as they have always been. There appears to be no breakthrough in the heavens, no magic cure for the problems of the world, no hero or deliverer on a white horse. What is now different is that because of Christ the world groans in expectation of that which is to be. There is an aching, a longing, almost a pregnancy, an even painful climate of anticipation and expectation, the resolution of which makes bearable the tribulations and trials of this moment. The very creation that appears so confident and permanent is longing for something better, and by that very longing has been set free from the rule of death and decay. There will be death, but it will be the death of the old order giving way to the new. It is that promise and hope that sustains the faithful even in the midst of the worst adversities of the world.

The substance of hope, then, consists in the expectation of what is, but what is is not yet but will surely be. That sounds like "church speak" until we realize that it is based upon the undeniable psychological truth that people live for and are sustained by their expectations. Destroy a people's expectations and you have destroyed the people. Conform people's expectations to the rapacious rule of what is, and you have cut them off, indeed subdued them to the point where they are already dead. Death is the absence of hope. Paul is saying that where there is hope there is life, and that where there is life, real life, and not merely existence, there is invariably hope. Thus, waiting is not a passive activity, something that occupies time and space before something "happens." Waiting is the fuel of hope. The essence of hope, said Paul, is waiting for that which is not but which is to be. The essence of the hope is our adoption as heirs of Christ. That has not yet been fully accomplished, but we wait for it. This is what he means, when beginning at verse 24, he writes, "For in this hope [that is, the waiting for the adoption as heirs of God with all that that implies] we were saved. Now hope that is seen is not hope. For who hopes for what he sees? But if we hope for what we do not see, we wait for it with patience." (Rom. 8:24-25).

This will be a hard sell to such an impatient people as we are, for whom instant gratification is a constitutional right and a psychological necessity. Our entitlement, impatience, and our materialism make it difficult for us to accept the reality of sufferings, the benefits of the long term over the short term, and a commitment to the things that we cannot see and cannot quantify. There is absolutely no escape from the crystal clear conclusion that it is exactly these imponderables, so out of character with American Christianity, to which we are summoned if we are in fact to be heirs of God and joint heirs with Christ. There is no way around this.

GOSPEL: JOHN 11:1-53

All the lectionaries call for the reading of John 11:1-53, and it will be tempting to make a nice narrative of the raising of Lazarus and of Jesus' encounter with his sisters Mary and Martha. Such a story will seem a blessed relief after the heavy theological diet of Ezekiel, Psalm 130, and Romans 8. Those who choose to preach from John 11 because it appears to be more user-friendly, are destined to underestimate the theological complexity of the gospel, and in so doing they will do great harm to the gospel, to themselves, and to their people.

The large and difficult questions with which we have been contending in the lessons for the Fifth Sunday in Lent are no less so here because they appear in narrative form peopled with familiar and much-loved personalities. Do not reduce this to a mere domestic parable, a feel-good Jesus story. John 11 will repay careful and conscientious reading, and every effort should be made to see the relationship of the issues in this narrative to those addressed elsewhere in the lections for this Sunday.

Death is the context of doubt. As long as there is life there is hope, goes the aphorism. But when life ends and death closes the door, doubt about life and faith and even hope itself enters in. Death is the essence of the dry bones. It is the ultimate depth of Psalm 130. Death is the logical end of the flesh, in Romans 8. Death now is the silent witness to the events of John 11. It is in the first instance the illness, and then the death of Lazarus of Bethany that commands our attention and that of Jesus. Verses 1-16 tell us of the illness of Lazarus, the entreaty to Jesus of the sisters Mary and Martha to visit and Jesus' delay in doing so, the actual death of Lazarus, and the decision of Jesus and the disciples to go to Bethany. This first section is puzzling on a number of points. First, we do not know if verse 3 ("So the sisters sent to him, saying, 'Lord, he whom you love is ill,' ") is meant to convey an invitation for Jesus to come and restore Lazarus to health, or an opportunity for Jesus to visit him in his illness, or before his death. We assume that the presence of Jesus was desired for some purpose, and we further assume that it was to either inhibit or to mediate the illness of which the sisters speak. They do not ask Jesus to come and heal their brother, nor do they ask him to prevent death. In fact, their message—"So the sisters sent to him"—asks nothing, but makes the statement, "Lord, he whom you love is ill." The implication of that statement is that the knowledge of that fact would impel Jesus to action, that is, to visit Bethany. We may infer even more from v. 32, where Mary remonstrates with Jesus upon his tardy arrival, with the words, "Lord, if you had been here, my brother would not have died."

Further difficulties in this section surround Jesus' reaction to the news of his friend's illness. First, at verse 4, he says, "This illness is not unto death; it is for the glory of God, so that the Son of God may be glorified by means of it." Then at verse 11, "Our friend Lazarus has fallen asleep, but I go to awake him out of sleep." We are confused, but so too are the disciples who think that Jesus means "sleep" and not death, but then Jesus says unambiguously at verse 14, "Lazarus is dead." His initial delay in returning to Bethany seems to be explained by his sense that the illness was not life-threatening. But now that Lazarus is dead, he says that for the sake of the disciples he was glad that he was not there, presumably so that they might have the benefit of witnessing the miracle which will confirm their faith. Jesus throughout appears to be manipulating the situation to his own purposes.

When Jesus enters Bethany he is greeted by the mourners, and by Martha, who says, "Lord, if you had been here my brother would not have died." Her sister will say the same thing at v. 32. Martha, however, adds to the remonstrance, "And even now I know that whatever you ask from God, God will give you." The situation is desperate, but not irreversible. "Your brother will rise again," says Jesus, and Martha says that she believes in the resurrection. Jesus, not content merely with a theological affirmation, says, "I am the resurrection and the life; he who believes in me, though he die, yet shall he live, and whoever lives and believes in me shall never die."

The theological becomes personal. Belief in a doctrine is not the same as belief in the one who is what the doctrine speaks of. Martha seems to "get it," that is, to understand both what is said and who said it, for when she announces to her sister that Jesus is nearby, she calls him teacher.

When Jesus meets Mary he joins in her weeping, and asks to be taken to the tomb where Lazarus was buried. Jesus wept; and this demonstration of affection and humanity produces a mixed result. Some say, "See how he loved him?" Others say, "Could not he who opened the eyes of the blind man have kept this man from dying?" This last rebuke is particularly bitter in that Jesus hardly knew the blind man at all, and Lazarus was an old friend. Why waste his powers on strangers?

From verses 38 to 44 we have the resurrection scene, a teaching device that Jesus arranges neither for the sake of himself, nor even for poor old Lazarus, but rather to display the power of God in the ultimate work of God: the creation of life. For the miracle to be real, and the source of that miracle, God, to be seen equally as real, the death of Lazarus must be real. He must be more than merely asleep. Martha, the practical sister, provides the affirmation of the reality of Lazarus' death by saying, "Lord, by this time there will be an odor, for he has been dead four days." The Authorized version puts it more plainly, "He stinketh"; and medieval artists loved to depict the crowd gathered before the tomb of Lazarus holding their noses against the anticipated stench. The prayer is for the benefit of the witnesses, and the resurrection itself is in two parts. First, Lazarus is called forth. Then to the crowd Jesus says, "Unbind him and let him go." Lazarus is thus both rescusitated and liberated. This twofold action is not unlike the reknitting of the bones, and the infusion of breath in Ezekiel 37.

The result of the miracle is mixed. Many are converted, but others become even more suspicious and hostile than they had been before. One who can raise the dead is not easily ignored. He is not subject to conventional ways or wisdom. He will carry the people before him, people easily persuaded by signs and miracles, and this will have such an unsteadying effect that the Romans will have to come to restore order. Caiaphas, the High Priest, prophesied that Jesus should die for the nation. His death would be a sacrifice for the nation and for the faithful scattered abroad. From that point the energies of the Sanhedrin were devoted to bringing this about.

The story is long and somewhat off-balance, with not one but two points of climax. *The* climax would appear to be the resurrection scene and the two commands. That is a scene not easily forgotten. But the fundamental focus of the story occurs earlier when Jesus makes his ultimate "I am" statement at verse 25, where he says to Martha, "I am the resurrection and the life." This statement, by which doctrine becomes personal, evokes Martha's confession at verse 27. She is now more than a friend, she is a believer. Others will be impressed with Jesus for what he did, and many followed him because he raised the dead. Martha is impressed with him for who he is, "the Christ, the Son of God, he who is coming into the world" (v. 27). Martha's confession and Jesus' identity can both be lost in the splendid detail of the raising of Lazarus, but here the resurrection is not an end in itself, but a means, pointing to the glory of God. Even after Lazarus is dead again, death is conquered by the giver of life. In the words of the ancient Easter prose, "He hath made captivity captive." The resurrection is not a personal immunization against death, and it is not the end of anything. It is the ultimate creative act of the creator-God, to whom is ascribed all glory, laud, and honor. These mighty acts reflect upon a mighty God. The people thus have every reason for thanksgiving, and for gratitude.

Prayer for the Preacher Preparing for the Fifth Sunday in Lent

O Lord Jesus Christ, Son of the living God: Grant
us so to feel and know thy love in thy passion, that
our hearts may be set on fire to love thee again, and
our brothers and sisters for thy sake; who livest and
reignest with the Father and the Holy Ghost, God, world
without end. Amen.

(Eric Milner-White, from *A Procession of Passion Prayers*)